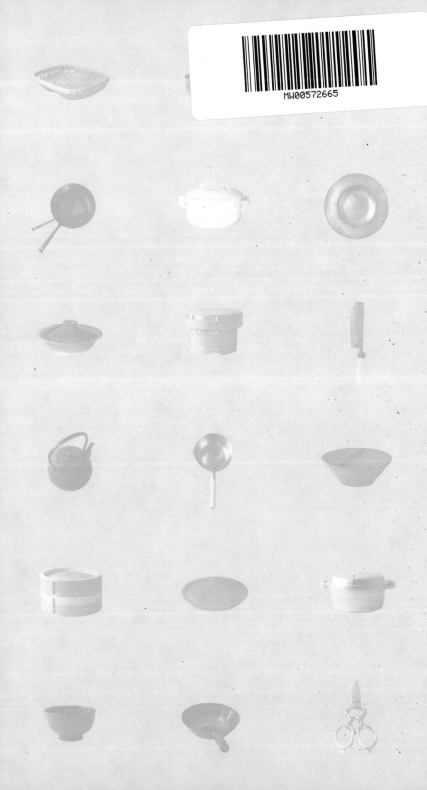

英語訳付き

受け継がれる職人・作家の手仕事

ニッポンの 台所道具と手入れ術

How to Care for Japanese Kitchen Utensils

日野明子

誠文堂新光社

はじめに

道具の手入れ。
昔はお母さんやおばあさんに習ったはずの普通のことが、
最近は伝わらなくなったといわれます。
私も母に教わらなかったひとりなのですが、
幸い、「作り手」という優秀な先生につけました。
使い方がわかると、使うのが楽しくなります。
使い込むってこういうことなのか、と納得します。
作り手から教えてもらったことを確認するために調べたところ、
化学に基づいていることに驚くことが多々ありました。
「素材を知る」。
これが、道具を使いこなす一番のポイントのようです。
「お手入れ」というと、
「きれいに保つこと」と、思われるかもしれません。
しかし、作り手からは
「新品同様に戻したらせっかくの使い込んだ味わいが台なし」
という言葉をよく聞きました。

使うことで、生まれる質感。
使い勝手にプラスして、これを楽しむことこそ、道具の醍醐味。

使いはじめたとき以上に良い道具になる。
この本が、そのお手伝いになれば幸いです。

日野明子

Preface

In older times, knowing how to care for kitchen utensils was something we were expected to learn from our mothers and grandmothers. These days it is harder to pass on this kind of everyday knowledge to younger generations. I also was not taught much by my mother about how to look after kitchen utensils, but have been fortunate to learn from excellent teachers – the makers of kitchenware. It is true that the more we learn about how to handle tools, the more we enjoy using them. We come to understand the beauty of tools that are well used and cared for. When doing some research on the information I gathered from the makers I visited, I was surprised to find that many of the things they told me were supported by theoretical chemistry. It seems that "to know its material" is the key to mastering the tool. "Taking care of tools" is sometimes understood to mean "keeping them neat and clean". However I have often heard the makers say, "You will spoil the charm of your well-used tool if you bring it back to brand new condition."

The texture and character of the tool develops as we use it over time. The true attraction of well-used tools lies in those added qualities as well as their practicality.

Your kitchen utensils can continue to improve and become better than when you first used them. If this book helps that happen, I would be more than happy.

Akiko Hino

Contents

木・竹の道具 Wooden & Bamboo Utensils

土の道具 Earthen Utensils

金属の道具 Metal Utensils

コラム Columns

※情報は2015年3月現在のものです。
※紹介している商品の取扱い店舗でも、
売り切れだったり、常に取扱っている
とは限りません。また、サイズなども
変更になることがありますので、店舗
で確認するようにしてください。
※This information is as of March, 2015.
※The products presented in this book
may be sold out or not be always
available at their stockists. Sizes and
other information are subject to change.
Please check at the store.

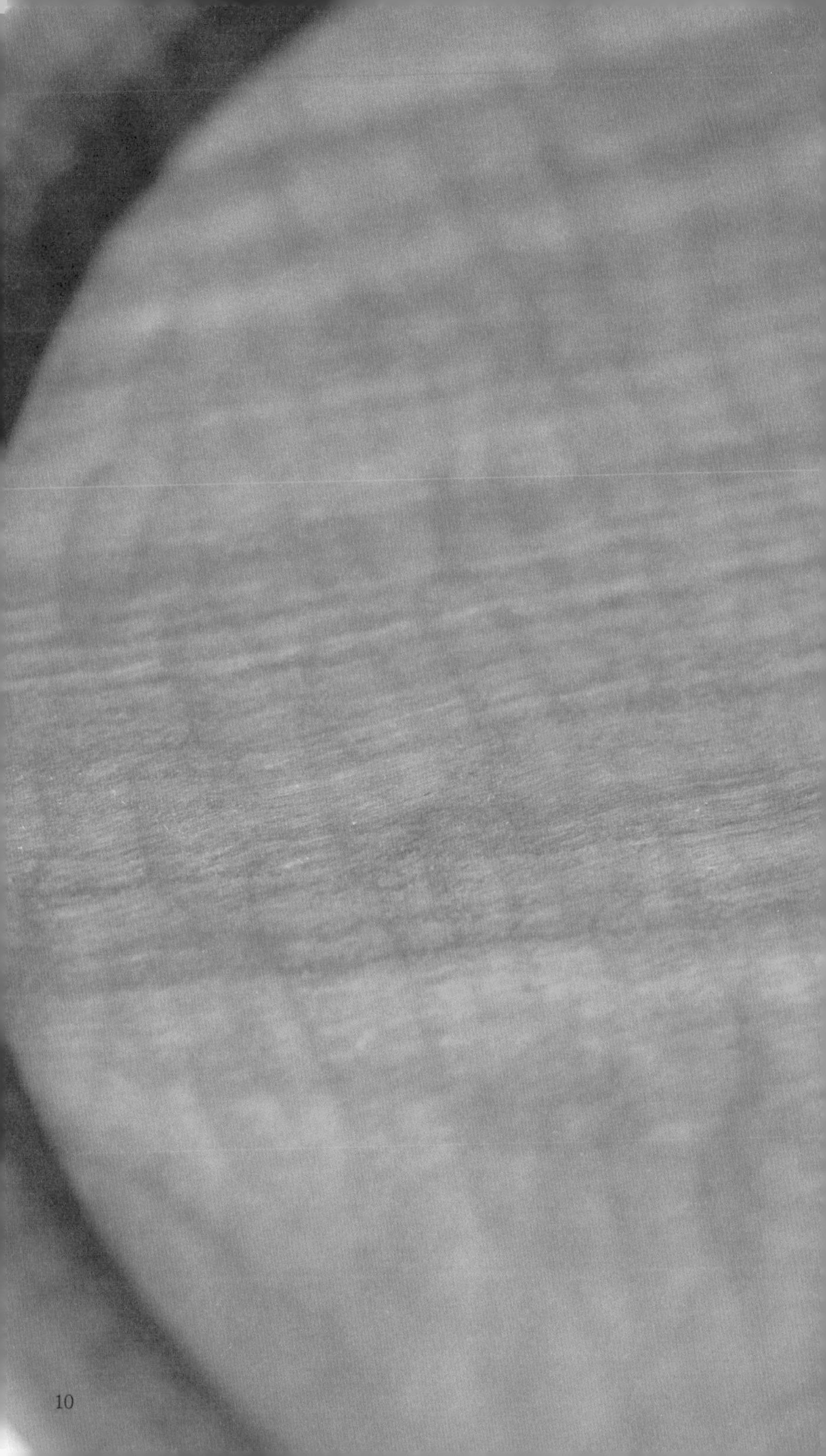

木・竹の道具
Wooden & Bamboo Utensils

日本は国土の7割が森のため、森林国といわれている。
台所道具にも、木や竹で作られているものは多い。
白木の皿などは一目瞭然だが、
曲げわっぱの弁当箱や、おひつ、まな板、
漆だって素地は木だ。
木や竹の道具は、「汚れる」のではなく「育つ」もの。
料理のシミも、手でさわったときにつく油も染み込んでいき、
それがなじんで味わい深くなっていく。
木や竹は伐採されて道具というかたちになったが、生き続けているのだ。

Japan is called a land of forests, as they cover seventy percent of the entire country. There are many Japanese kitchen items made of wood and bamboo including: unvarnished plates, cutting boards, magewappa (bentwood) lunch boxes and ohitsu (a container for cooked rice). The body of urushi ware (Japanese lacquerware) is also wood. Wooden utensils do not get "dirty", they simply "mature" over time. Stains from cooking and natural hand oils from touching become a part of their character. Wood and bamboo, although it is no longer in its original state, continues to live when transformed into tools and utensils.

川端健夫の

白木の器

Shiraki Unvarnished Woodenware / Takeo Kawabata

菓子盆9寸　Cake Tray (27cm)

素材 Material	チェリー Cherry wood
サイズ Dimensions	直径27×高さ2.2cm D27 x H2.2cm
主な取扱い店	ギャラリー・マンマミーア KOHORO スパイラルマーケット CLASKA Gallery & Shop "DO" 日本橋店
Stockists	gallery-mamma mia KOHORO Spiral Market CLASKA Gallery & Shop "DO" Nihonbashi

その他のラインナップ　Product Information

木材はほかに、ウォールナット、クリ、ナラ、クルミがある。菓子盆は6
～10寸のサイズ展開あり。ランチプレート、パスタ皿、スコーンプレート、
カトラリーなど、多数のアイテムがある。

The products are also made of walnut, chestnut, oak and kurumi
(Japanese walnut). The cake tray is available in various sizes from 18cm
to 30cm in diameter. Many other products are available including lunch
plates, pasta plates, scone plates and cutlery.

白木の器といえどもほとんどの場合、オイルが塗られている。塗装は汚れをつきにくくするために行うが、木の反りを防ぐためでもある。川端健夫さんの器には、蜜蝋とエゴマ油の塗装がされているが、それでも、使い込んでいくうちに、カサカサしてくることもある。「しまい込まずに、毎日でも使ってほしい」と川端さんは言うが、それは、そうすることで適度な水分と油分を与えるという意味。木肌がカサついてきたら、油を塗ること。しかし、油の種類によってはベトベトしたまま乾かない。川端さんは、さらっとした仕上がりがべたつかないエゴマ油をすすめている。

白木の器は、水がついたままだとカビが生えたり、腐る原因になる。使ったら、しっかり乾かすこと。これが最も重要。といっても、お日様に当てるのは厳禁。日光はとても強いため、直射日光に当てると、急速に水分が失われ、木は反ったり割れたりしてしまう。乾燥した場所でも反りや割れは生じる。過度な水分は腐る元だが、使って洗うを繰り返しながらの適度な湿気は不可欠だ。

どんなものでも「慣らし」は必要。オイル仕上げの白木の器も、使い込んでいくうちになじんでいく。使いはじめから醤油やトマトペーストなど、色が濃いものをのせると、木に染み込んでしまう。シミが気になる人は、最初のうちは色が濃いものはのせないほうがいい。

Although shiraki means unvarnished wood, most shiraki woodenware is treated with oil. The oil coating protects the wood from stains and prevents warping. Takeo Kawabata uses beeswax and egoma oil (perilla seed oil) for his woodenware but the wood can still dry out with use. "I want my woodenware to be used every day instead of stored away," says Takeo, so that it absorbs a little moisture and oil from its surrounding environment. When the surfaces of the wood get rough and dry, you can re-treat them with oil. Just remember some oils are too oily to dry out. Takeo recommends egoma oil for a light, not-too-greasy finish.

If any water is left on the surface, the shiraki wood tends to mold or decay. Make sure to dry completely after every use. Having said that, the shiraki should not be exposed to the sun. Strong direct sunlight will make the wood lose its moisture too quickly and that will cause warping or cracking. This also can happen in extremely dry places. While having excessive moisture can cause the wood decay, keeping the wood at the right level of humidity by repeated washing and drying is essential.

Any new kitchen utensils need to "be conditioned". The texture of the shiraki woodenware will improve with use. If you place the dark-colored sauces like soy sauce or tomato paste in your new woodenware, they will seep into the wood grain. To avoid staining, it is better not to use these sauces until your woodenware has had some use.

日々の手入れ Daily care

使う前
Before use

盛りつける前は、盛る面を濡れ布巾で
さっと拭くことで、シミを防ぐことがで
きる。

Before placing food, give the plate a quick
wipe with a damp cloth to prevent food
stains.

3 泡をしっかりと流したら、乾いた布
巾で拭く。

After rinsing off the suds thoroughly
wipe the plate with a dry cloth.

使った後
After use

1 油が気にならないときは、ぬるま湯
だけで洗い流す。

If the plate is not too greasy, just wash
with lukewarm water.

4 拭いてからすぐにはしまわない。立
て掛けてひと晩くらいは乾かす。

Do not put the plate away immediately
after wiping. Prop it up and air dry at
least overnight.

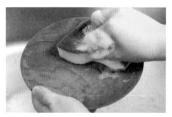

2 油が気になる場合は、スポンジに
中性洗剤を泡立てて洗う。

If the plate is greasy, wash with a sudsy
mild detergent and a sponge.

5 オープン棚など、常に空気が流れ
ているところに置くのがベスト。

The best place to keep the wooden
ware is on an open shelf or a place with
good airflow.

特別な手入れ Occasional care

木に潤いを与える
Moistening the wood

1 木肌がカサついたときは、キッチンペーパーにエゴマ油などの乾性油を染み込ませ、器全体にたっぷり塗る。

When the wood surface feels rough and dry, dip a paper towel in a drying oil such as egoma oil (perilla seed oil) and apply generously on all the surfaces of the plate.

2 新しいキッチンペーパーで余分な油を拭き取る。

Wipe the excess oil with fresh paper towels.

3 立て掛けて、油分をしっかりと乾かす。

Prop up the plate and let the oil dry completely.

困ったときは Troubleshooting

木肌がケバケバしてきたとき
Dry and rough surfaces

1 サンドペーパー（＃400程度）をA4サイズの1/8くらいにカットし、3つ折りにする。

Cut a sheet of sandpaper (grit of about 400) to about 1/8 A4 paper size. Fold it in three.

2 木目に沿って、1のサンドペーパーをなでる程度の力でかける。

Sand the wood very gently in the direction of the grain.

やってはいけないこと
DON'TS

| 電子レンジ Microwave | 食洗機 Dishwasher | 金属タワシ Metallic scrubber | 天日干し Dry in direct sunlight |
| 冷蔵庫 Keep in the refrigerator | 浸け置き Soak in water | | |

白木の器の作り手を訪ねる

川端健夫さん

Visiting Takeo Kawabata / Maker of shiraki unvarnished woodenware

　昔、養蚕場だった築80年の木造の建物では、夫が木工をし、妻が菓子を作っている。農業を学び、農業の仕事に就いていた川端健夫さんは、ひょんなことから木工の職業訓練校に入り、そこから木と向き合うことに。当初は家具作家だったが、子どもができたことをきっかけに、木のスプーンを作ってみることにした。しかし、子どもにこのスプーンでミルクを飲ませようとしても、なかなか飲んでくれない。あげる方も飲む方もへとへとになったとき、「片口だと飲ませやすい」とアドバイスをもらう。そこで作ったのが片口の小さな器。赤ん坊の小さな口にミルクが自然に流れ込んでくる片口は、とても飲みやすかったようで、ぐんぐん飲んでくれたそうだ。

　川端さんが家具を作りはじめたときは「とにかくカッコイイものを」と、使いやすさそっちのけにしていたそうだが、器やスプーンを気持ちよく使ってくれる家族を見て、使いやすく、長く使い続けられるものを作るようになった。もちろん、自分でもしっかり使って試してみる。器は口に入る食べ物がのるもの。だから、自然のものを使いたいと、蜜蝋とエゴマ油で塗装している。この特製オイルで、木の色がグンと浮き立ってくる器ができあがるようになったのだ。

In an 80-year-old timber building, which used be a silk farm factory, the husband does woodwork and his wife makes pastries. Takeo Kawabata studied agriculture and worked in that business. After an unexpected turn of events, he went to vocational school to learn woodworking and has been engaged in it ever since. Takeo worked as a furniture maker at first. When his son was born he tried making a wooden spoon. He scooped milk in the spoon and tried to feed his baby son but that did not work. When both the father and son were exhausted after a series of unsuccessful attempts, someone said to him, "It is easy to feed using a lipped cup." Takeo made a small lipped cup and tried it out. The milk flew easily in to the baby's little mouth and he kept drinking.

　Takeo used to concentrate on "stylish designs" in making furniture, not on functionality, but his focus shifted when he saw his family enjoy using his handmade cutlery and tableware at home. He started to make products that were practical and also long-lasting. Now Takeo tries his new products by himself. He wants his wooden vessels to be safe enough to eat from and uses beeswax and egoma oil for coating. This specially mixed oil brings out the beautiful colors in his woodenware.

1.川端さんは椅子の脚などを作るための旋盤で、皿を作っている。この道具を見ると、家具出身とわかる。2.家具を作るための鉋の数々。3.こちらは家具の型紙。4.小高い丘の上に建つ建物に、川端さんの工房とギャラリー、奥さんの美愛さんのパティスリーとカフェがある。

1.Takeo makes his plates on a lathe usually used for making chair legs and the like. The equipment is a reminder of Takeo's earlier career as a furniture maker. 2.Hand planes for furniture making. 3.Templates for furniture. 4.Takeo's workshop and gallery, and his wife Mia's patisserie and café, are in a building on a small hill.

1.さじだけでなく、手間のかかるフォークも作っている。木のフォークであれば器に傷がつかないから、漆の器でパスタも食べられる。2.器を作るきっかけとなった授乳スプーンと片口。落として少し欠けているが、それもいい思い出。3.付き合いのあるガラス作家の木下宝さんと川端さんの蓋とさじを合わせたシュガーボウル。4.奥さんの美愛さんが営むパティスリーではケーキや焼き菓子をカフェでも提供している。菓子盆は焼き菓子のディスプレーにも使用。

1.Takeo produces not only spoons but also forks, which are more time consuming to make. A wooden fork does not scratch the surface so you can use it to eat pasta from an urushi bowl. 2.The feeding spoon and lipped bowl that motivated Takeo to make tableware. Even a chip on the rim is a fond memory. 3.A collaboration with his fellow craftsman, glass artist Takara Kinoshita. Takeo made a lid and spoon to match Takara's glass sugar bowl. 4.Takeo's wife Mia runs a patisserie and you can enjoy her cakes and sweets at her café. Takeo's tray is used to display Mia's baked sweets.

作り手の使い方

美愛さんのカフェでは、もちろん川端さんの皿とカトラリーが使われる。バターの入ったケーキも、カスタードクリームももちろん大丈夫。使い込んだものを見ると、自分でも使いたくなる。

How the makers use it

Takeo's plates and cutlery are the obvious choice for Mia's café. From buttery cakes to custard, wooden plates can be used for anything. When you see well-loved plates like these, it makes you feel like using them at home as well.

木屋の

まな板

Manaita Cutting Board / Kiya

木曽ひのき まな板（一枚板）
Kiso Hinoki (Japanese cypress) Manaita Cutting Board (single plate)

サイズ Dimensions	横42×縦18×高さ3cm W42 x L18 x H3cm
主な取扱い店	日本橋 木屋本店 木屋玉川店 木屋大丸梅田店 木屋東武池袋店 木屋博多大丸福岡天神店 木屋大丸東京店
Stockists	Kiya Nihonbashi Main Store Kiya Tamagawa Kiya Daimaru Umeda Kiya Tobu Ikebukuro Kiya Hakata Daimaru Fukuoka Tenjin Kiya Daimaru Tokyo

その他のラインナップ Product Information

まな板はほかにイチョウの素材もあり、さまざまなサイズがある。包丁、料理ばさみ、おろし金、銅鍋、アルミ鍋、鉄器製品など多数のアイテムがある。

The cutting board is also available in Icho (ginkgo wood) and comes in various sizes. Many other products are available including hocho knives, kitchen scissors, graters, copper pots, aluminum pots and ironware.

「刃物の木屋」という看板を背負った木屋さんに、まな板のことを伺うのは失礼かと思ったが、包丁の女房役なのだからと、お邪魔してみた。だが、それは正解だった。「包丁を一番痛めないのは、空で切ることですよ」。木屋の石田克由さんとは、こんな冗談めいた話からはじまった。要は、刃を受け止める際の衝撃が大きいと刃に悪い、ということだ。

弾力と適度な柔らかさがある木のまな板が良いが、堅い木は厳禁。刃こぼれしてしまう恐れがある上に、包丁を持つ手も反発で疲れてくる。油分を含むので水はけが良く、復元力もある、イチョウがまず一番。そして抗菌効果があり腐食にも強いヒノキ、切切れが良く、乾燥しやすいホウなどが続く。

さて、私のまな板は、気づいたら木口がカビだらけだった。「水洗いが足りないんですよ」と石田さん。洗剤すら、洗い残しはカビを誘発するという。おすすめはクレンザーなどの磨き粉でしっかり洗い、磨き粉の粒一つ残らないように流すこと。「お皿を洗う2倍の時間はかけてください」。驚きだが、これが目安。そして、しっかり乾かし、風が通るところに置いておく。

I was wondering if it would be rude to visit Kiya, the store that prides itself on selling quality knives, to ask about cutting boards instead of knives. But cutting boards were important for hocho knives I thought. They are like their faithful assistant. So I went to Kiya, and it turned out that I was right. Katsuyoshi Ishida from Kiya started his explanation with a joke. "The best way to protect hocho knives is to use them in the air." What he meant was; the bigger the impact of hitting the board, the bigger the damage to the blade.

The wood that has good impact resistance and moderate softness makes a good cutting board. Hard wood should never be used for a cutting board because it damages or nicks the blade. Cutting against a hard surface also tires your arm. Taking this into account, the best wood for a cutting board is Icho (ginkgo wood). It has oily properties that protect the wood and good resilience. Next best are Hinoki (Japanese cypress) for its antibacterial properties and resistance to rotting and Ho (Japanese white bark magnolia) for its low water retention and quick-to-dry nature.

One time I was shocked to find my cutting board covered with mold on the sides. "That is because you did not rinse it long enough," said Mr. Ishida. Any left residue, even detergent, can cause mold to form. The recommended washing method is to scrub the cutting board with an abrasive cleanser and rinse thoroughly until every trace of cleanser is gone. "Wash your cutting board twice as long as you wash dishes," advised Mr. Ishida. Quite surprising, but that is the standard. Dry thoroughly and leave in a well-ventilated place.

日々の手入れ Daily care

使う前
Before use

1 水で流すと、食材のにおいや細菌などがつきにくくなる。

Rinsing the cutting board under running water reduces food odor and the risk of bacteria forming on the surface.

2 しっかり拭くというより、さっとでOK。

A quick wipe is sufficient.

使った後
After use

1 タワシにクレンザー（粉末タイプ）をつける。

Apply a powder cleanser on a tawashi or a scrubbing brush.

2 タワシでゴシゴシこすり洗いをする。

Scrub down the cutting board.

3 忘れがちな木口の部分もしっかりとこすり洗いする。

Make sure to scrub all sides.

特別な手入れ Occasional care

脱臭と漂白に
Deodorizing and bleaching

ときどき輪切りにしたレモンでこすると、脱臭と漂白を兼ねた効果がある。

Rub the cutting board with a cut lemon occasionally. Lemon acts as bleach and a deodorizer.

4 すすぎ残りがないように、長めの時間をかけてすすぐ。木口も忘れずに。

Rinse the cutting board very thoroughly so that no residue will be left. Make sure to rinse the sides as well.

5 布巾で拭き、ある程度水分を取ってから乾かす。

Wipe dry with a cloth.

6 木目に沿って立てて置く。半分に切ったワインのコルクなどをかませて空気が通るようにし、ときどき上下を逆にして置くといい。

Stand the cutting board on the legs of wine cork cut in half for good airflow. Stand the board's grain vertically. Turn the cutting board upside down occasionally.

やってはいけないこと
DON'TS

電子レンジ Microwave	食洗機 Dishwasher	金属タワシ Metallic scrubber	天日干し Dry in direct sunlight
冷蔵庫 Keep in the refrigerator			

柴田慶信商店の

曲げわっぱ

Magewappa (bentwood ware) / Shibata Yoshinobu Shoten

きこり弁当箱	Kikori Lunch Box (woodcutter's lunch box)
素材 Material	秋田杉 Akita cedar
サイズ Dimensions	本体:直径12×高さ8cm　中子:直径12×高さ4.5cm Outer container: D12 x H8cm　Inner container: D12 x H4.5cm
主な取扱い店	柴田慶信商店 本店 柴田慶信商店 浅草店 POST DETAIL Analogue Life FRANK暮らしの道具 HANAわくすい
Stockists	Shibata Yoshinobu Shoten Main Store Shibata Yoshinobu Shoten Asakusa POST DETAIL Analogue Life FRANK kurashi no dougu HANA-Wakusui

その他のラインナップ Product Information

弁当箱は小判弁当、丸弁当など。その他におひつ(P27)、飯台、和蒸篭(P31)、パン皿なども
ある。

The magewappa lunch box is available in oval, round and other shapes. Other products
available include ohitsu (Page 27), handai (wooden barrel for sushi rice), Japanese seiro
(Page 31) and bread plates.

曲げわっぱは、秋田県大館の伝統的工芸品。秋田杉を木目に沿って薄くそいだ板を湯通しし、柔らかくして曲げて側面を作り、底をつけたもの。弁当箱やおひつなどに使われる、江戸時代から続く技法だ。本来は塗装をせずに作ることで、天然秋田杉の吸湿性や殺菌効果でご飯の水分をほどよく吸水し、冷めてもおいしく傷みにくくする良さがあるのだが、80年代後半になると、シミを嫌がる消費者のために、ウレタンなどで塗装する作り手がほとんどになった。だが、それではご飯の水分は取れない。柴田さんは、無塗装こそがご飯をおいしくするという信念のもと、一貫して無塗装を貫いてきた。

2代目の昌正さんが使っている弁当箱はすごい。美しく木目が浮き出ている。「クレンザーを使って、木目に沿って柔らかい部分を削り取るように、ものすごく力を入れて洗うんです」と教えてくれた。また、黒ズミになった場合、それは自然の経過。気にする必要はなく、使い続けていいと言う。

ちなみに、私は曲げわっぱの弁当箱を余りご飯のおひつ代わりに使っている。プラスチック容器だと冷蔵庫から出して蓋を開けると水滴が落ち、ご飯がガチガチに固くなるのに比べ、曲げわっぱに入れたご飯は、いい感じに湿度を保ち、冷めていてもとてもおいしいのだ。

Magewappa (bentwood) is a traditional craft from Odate City, Akita Prefecture. Local Akita sugi (cedar) is thinly stripped along the grain and boiled to bend into circle to form the sidewall, and attached to the base. This technique has been used to make containers such as bento lunch boxes and ohitsu (a container for cooked rice) since the Edo period, more than four hundred years ago. Magewappa wares made in the traditional way have no protective coating and the Akita cedar's ability to absorb moisture and disinfecting properties are fully utilized to keep cooked rice fresh and tasty even after it gets cold. In the late 1980s, most magewappa makers started to use a urethane coating in response to consumers' dislike for staining. The coating, however, prevents the magewappa wares from absorbing moisture. Shibata Yoshinobu Shoten, magewappa maker, has been making non-coated magewappa products with a strong belief that uncoated bare wood is the key to enhancing the taste of cooked rice.

Yoshinobu's son, Yoshimasa, has a magewappa lunch box with amazingly defined grain. "I use a powder cleanser to wash my lunch box. I scrub with the grain very hard, almost like shaving the surface," Yoshimasa said. The darkening of the wood is a natural process and there is no need to worry, he added.

I use my magewappa lunch box to keep cooked rice. I find the rice kept in a plastic container is so hard when taken out of the refrigerator and water droplets drip on the rice from the lid. The rice in the magewappa lunch box, on the other hand, stays moist and tastes good even when eaten cold.

日々の手入れ Daily care

使う前
Before use

1 色がつきやすいものを入れるとき
　　は、水で濡らす。

When placing food that could leave
color stains, wet the inside of the
container with water.

3 水でクレンザーをよくすすいだら、
　　布巾で水気を拭く。熱めの湯です
　　すぐと乾きが早い。

After rinsing off the cleanser
thoroughly with water, wipe dry with a
cloth. Rinsing with hot water will help
the container dry faster.

使った後
After use

1 水を流して汚れを浮かせる。

Run water inside the container to
loosen any stuck on food.

4 水分がこもらないように、内側を
　　外に向けてしっかり乾かす。

Dry the container with its inside facing
to the open air so that no moisture
stays in the container.

2 タワシにクレンザー（粉末タイプ）
　　をつけ、力を入れてゴシゴシ洗う。

Scrub the container with a tawashi or
a scrubbing brush and with a powder
cleanser.

やってはいけないこと
DON'TS

| 電子レンジ Microwave | 食洗機 Dishwasher | 金属タワシ Metallic scrubber | 天日干し Dry in direct sunlight |
| 冷蔵庫 Keep in the refrigerator | 重曹 Baking soda | | |

木・竹の道具 ……… 曲げわっぱ

右が曲げわっぱのおひつで、左が桶のおひつ。曲げわっぱは、1枚の板を曲げて作るため、木の長さによって直径が制限される。桶は、短冊状の板をくっつけて作るため、いくらでも大きなものを作ることができるが、逆に小さいものだと、厚みばかりが出て内容量が少なくなってしまう。曲げわっぱのおひつ（右）／柴田慶信商店、桶のおひつ（左）／ゆかい社中そらぐみ

Magewappa-ohitsu, right and Oke-ohitsu, left. The magewappa is made by bending a strip of wood and the diameter of the container is limited by the length of the wood. The oke is constructed by joining wooden slats and it can be made as big as desired. However, the thick wood decreases the inner capacity, which is a drawback for making smaller containers. Magewappa-ohitsu (right) / Shibata Yoshinobu Shoten, Oke-ohitsu (left) / Yukaishachu Soragumi

曲げわっぱと桶
Magewappa and Oke

　白木のおひつを使おうと思った際、2つの選択肢がある。曲げわっぱと桶だ。
　この2つは、作り方が決定的に異なる。曲げわっぱは、木を繊維に沿って切って板状にしたものを使う。その板を湯煎して曲げ、1周した重なりを桜の皮などで縫い留めて作る。一方、桶は短冊状の板を横につなげ、たがで締める。側面同士をくっつけていくので、短冊にある程度の厚みが必要になり、弁当箱のような小さいものを作るのには向いていない。

When it comes to choosing unvarnished ohitsu (a container for cooked rice) there are two different styles. Magewappa and oke.
　The defining difference between the two is the way they are constructed. The magewappa container is made of a strip of wood that is cut along its fiber. It is boiled to bend into a circular shape and tied up at the overlapping area with bark from cherry blossom. The oke container is made by joining rectangular wooden slats and binding them together with hoops. Because the wood needs to be relatively thick, this method makes it unsuitable for smaller containers such as lunch boxes.

照宝の

中華蒸篭

Chinese Seiro (Chinese steamer) / Shouhou

中華蒸篭 直径30cm
Chinese Seiro (Chinese steamer) 30cm in diameter

素材	杉
Material	Cedar
サイズ	直径30×高さ7.5cm×2段
Dimensions	D30 x H7.5cm x 2tier
主な取扱い店	照宝
Stockist	Shouhou

その他のラインナップ Product Information

素材は杉以外に、檜（国産）、白木、竹がある。サイズは直径10〜60cmの18種
類。どのサイズの蒸篭にも使える蒸し板や、蒸篭用の布巾、中華鍋のほか、
多種多様の中華調理道具がある。

The seiro steamer is also available in hinoki (Japanese cypress), shiraki
(unvarnished wood) and bamboo and comes in 18 sizes from 10 cm to
60 cm in diameter. Steaming rings for all sizes, cloths for seiro, wok and
a wide range of utensils for Chinese cooking are also available.

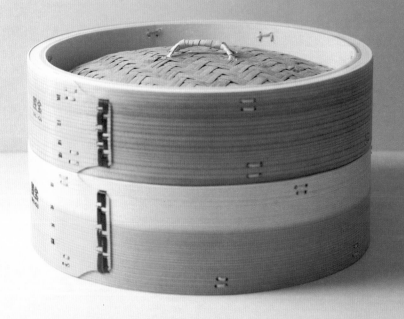

照宝の店長である永井正人さんに手入れ方法を尋ねたら、「手入れなんて必要ないですよ」との答えが返ってきた。中華蒸篭は「洗ってはいけない」。疑い深く、中華の料理人に蒸篭の使い方を尋ねたら「洗いませんよ。壊れちゃいますから」と、当然のように答えが返ってきた。よくよく考えると、蒸篭は「蒸気を出して使う、蒸す道具」だ。蒸気＝消毒をしながら使っている、と考えれば、洗う必要がないことがわかる。

中華蒸篭は、薄くスライスした竹や木をぐるぐると廻して作る。この何重かに巻いている重なり部分の一枚一枚の間は、厳密にいうと隙間が空いている。だから、洗えば当然隙間に水が入る。この水が完全に乾くのには、相当な時間がかかるため、乾く前にカビが生える可能性が出てくるのだ。

蒸篭を使えば、100度の蒸気があがる。「100度の蒸気は消毒作用があるのだから、わざわざ洗う必要がない」というのが、中華蒸篭の手入れ不要の論法なのだ。

中華料理屋さんが「壊れちゃう」と言ったのも、隙間に水が入ることを指したのだろう。竹や木の隙間に水分が入ったままだと、素材はゆるみ、そして傷み、それを続けていけば壊れてしまう。至極単純なことなのだ。どうしても汚れが気になる人は、布巾やクッキングシート、またはお皿を敷いて、その上に食材をのせるといい。使用後は、濡れ布巾などで拭けばきれいになる。

When I asked Masato Nagai, the manager at Shouhou, a Chinese cookware store, about how to care for Chinese seiro he said, "You don't need to do anything." He meant Chinese seiro "should not be washed". Not totally convinced, I went to ask a Chinese chef the same question. "I don't wash them. They will break if I do," he answered as if that was obvious. Actually, seiro always is used for steaming and that means it gets disinfected while being used. If we look at it this way, the idea of not cleaning actually makes sense.

The seiro is made by bending a thin strip of wood or bamboo into a circular shape to make several layers, and there is a tiny gap created between each layer. If the seiro is washed, water seeps through these gaps. It takes quite some time for the trapped moisture in these gaps to completely dry out. This means there is a chance for mold to form.

When you cook with the seiro, it is steamed at 100 degrees. "The steam kills germs in the seiro, so there is no need to wash it" is the logic behind this no-fuss method of seiro care.

The Chinese chef who said "they will break" was probably referring to the trapped moisture between the gaps. The seiro, whether made of wood or bamboo, will soften because of this moisture, get damaged and eventually become unusable. It is quite simple. If you are still worried about your seiro getting dirty, line the base with a cloth or baking paper, or set a small dish in it before placing cooking ingredients. Wipe your seiro with a damp cloth to clean after use.

使いはじめ Before first use

1 蒸篭をのせる鍋（または中華鍋）で湯を沸かす。

Boil water in a saucepan or wok.

2 1の鍋が沸騰したら蒸篭をのせて15分ほど空蒸しすると、木の独特のにおいが消える。鍋と蒸篭のサイズが合わない場合は、中央に穴があいた蒸し板（別売り）を使うとよい。

Set the seiro on top of the saucepan. Let the steam through for about 15 minutes. This removes the new wood smell. If the seiro does not sit well on the pan, mushiita, an aluminum steaming ring (sold separately at Shouhou store), can be used. The ring helps the seiro sit securely and allows the steam through at the same time.

日々の手入れ Daily care

使うとき
Before placing food

すのこを汚さないよう、クッキングシートや皿などを敷いて使う。

Line the base of the steamer with baking paper or place a small plate to keep the sunoko (slats at the base) clean.

使った後
After use

使用後は水に浸けたりしないこと。湿らせた布巾で拭くだけでOK。

Do not soak the seiro in water after use. Cleaning with a damp cloth is sufficient.

やってはいけないこと
DON'TS

電子レンジ Microwave	食洗機 Dishwasher	金属タワシ Metallic scrubber	天日干し Dry in direct sunlight
冷蔵庫 Keep in the refrigerator			

ビニール袋など、通気性の悪いものに入れてしまうのは避ける。
Avoid storing the seiro in a plastic bag or anything air tight.

木
・
竹
の
道
具
………
中
華
蒸
篭

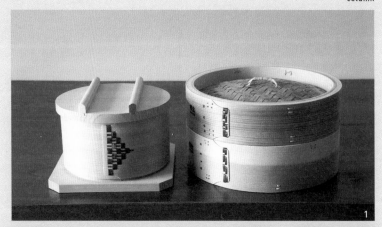

1.右が中華蒸篭で、左が和蒸篭。竹で編んだ蓋の中華蒸篭
は、蒸気を逃がすため、水滴が食材に落ちにくい。木の蓋の
和蒸篭は、蒸気を閉じ込めるため、おこわや水分を逃したく
ない野菜などに向く。2.右の中華蒸篭は薄い板を何重かに巻
いて作られ、左の和蒸篭は薄い板1枚を曲げて作られている。
中華蒸篭(右)／照宝、和蒸篭(左)／柴田慶信商店

1.Chinese seiro, right and Japanese seiro, left. The bamboo
woven lid allows steam through and keeps condensation
from dripping on the food. The wooden lid is suitable for cooking okowa (steamed sticky rice) and
vegetables that you prefer to cook in their own juices. 2.The Chinese seiro on right is constructed by
bending a thin strip into the tight circle to make several layers. The Japanese seiro on left is made by
bending a single thin strip into a circular shape.
Chinese seiro (right) / Shouhou, Japanese seiro (left) / Shibata Yoshinobu Shoten

中華蒸篭と和蒸篭
Chinese seiro and Japanese seiro

　蒸篭には2つのタイプがあるといわれたら、一瞬何のことかと疑問に思う人も多いだろ
う。私自身もそうだった。でもよく考えてみたら、蓋が編んであるものと、木のものがある
ことを思い出した。竹を編んだ状態のものが中華蒸篭で、木の蓋が和蒸篭。蓋の構造の
違いは、蒸気に関係する。中華蒸篭は蒸気を逃がし、和蒸篭は逃さないで閉じ込める。

　底の部分も異なる。中華蒸篭は底が一体化しているが、和蒸篭は取り外しのできるす
のこが置いてある。また、中華蒸篭は何段にも重ねられ、どの段も蒸し上がりは変わらな
い。一方、和蒸篭は深さがあるため、茶碗蒸しなど高さのあるものも蒸せる。

If someone said, "There are two types of seiro steamer," many people would be doubtful for a second. I
was also doubtful at first but when I thought about it carefully, I remembered there were Chinese seiro
with a woven lid and Japanese seiro with a wooden lid. The difference in the structure of the lids affects
the way they steam. While the Chinese seiro allows steam to escape, the Japanese seiro traps it in.

　Their bases are also different. The base of the Chinese seiro is unified with the body part and
the Japanese seiro has a removable sunoko base (slatted mat). Each seiro has its advantages: the
Chinese seiro can be stacked one on top of another and the food in each steamer is cooked evenly.
The Japanese seiro is deep enough to cook food in a cup such as Chawanmushi (Japanese savory egg
custard often served in individual cups).

ゆかい社中そらぐみの

桶細工のおひつ

Oke-Ohitsu (Wooden Container for Cooked Rice)
Yukaishachu Soragumi

司製樽さんのおひつ　3合半
Tsukasaseitaru Ohitsu 3.5 rice-cooker cups (1 cup =180cc)

素材 Materials	木曽椹（天然）、銅 Kiso sawara cypress wood (natural), copper
サイズ Dimensions	直径18×高さ14㎝（蓋の直径20.5㎝） D18 x H14㎝ (Lid diameter 20.5㎝)
主な取扱い店	jokogumo OUTBOUND まちのシューレ963 ゆかい社中そらぐみ
Stockists	jokogumo OUTBOUND Machino-schule 963 Yukaishachu Soragumi

その他のラインナップ Product Information
おひつは5合サイズもある。両サイズとも「ゆかい社中そらぐみ」
のプロデュースの元で、司製樽が製造している。

Ohitsu for 5 rice-cooker cups is also available. Both ohitsu are produced
by Tsukasaseitaru and marketed by "Yukaishachu Soragumi".

桶は直しながら使うものだ。桶細工の材料である木は生きている。呼吸しているのだから、プラスチックのようにかたちが変わらない、ということはない。充分に乾燥させた木を使っていれば収縮は少ないが、急激な湿度の差によっては、伸び縮みする。大きく縮んだ場合、ことわざにもあるが「たがが外れる」ことになる。これは、竹や金具の留め具が外れること。元に戻すこともできるが、木の縮みが大きいと外れが癖になる。そんなときは、桶屋に持っていって調整してもらっていた。汚れたら削り直しもしてもらえる。桶とはそうやって使うものなのだ。

炊いたご飯を入れるとご飯の余分な水分を吸い取り、味や固さが良いあんばいになる桶細工のおひつ。使うときは、濡らさずに使う。実は、ほかの作り手の多くは「炊いたご飯を入れる前に、水にさらすか、濡れ布巾で拭いてから使うように」と言うが、司製樽の原田啓司さんは「濡らさずに炊きたてのご飯を入れてください」と言う。おひつは、ご飯の水分を調節するために存在するのだから、わざわざ水分の吸い取りを悪くする必要はないだろうというのだ。私もまったく同意見だ。

Oke, a Japanese flat-bottomed wooden tub, is made to last for many years, being repaired by the maker when needed. Unlike plastic, wood is an organic material and changes its volume by absorbing and releasing moisture. A well dried oke does not shrink much but can expand or contract with humidity swings. If the contraction of the wood is too much, the hoop around the oke will come off. It can be placed back but will get loose again if the shrinkage is excessive. In older times, the oke was taken to oke-ya, oke makers, for repair. The oke-ya would adjust the hoop and shave the worn-out surfaces clean. This is how the oke should be looked after.

When oke-ohitsu (oke-style container for cooked rice) is used for freshly cooked rice, it absorbs excess moisture making the taste and texture of the rice just right. The ohitsu should not be wetted before use. Many ohitsu makers advise to immerse it in water or wipe with a damp cloth but Keiji Harada from Tsukasasei Taru suggests, "Just put freshly cooked rice straight in without wetting the ohitsu." He explains that the ohitsu is supposed to absorb excess moisture, so wetting the inside will make it less effective. I totally agree.

使いはじめ Before first use

1 水を入れて、全体を軽くすすぐように
にして流す。

Rinse the inside of the ohitsu with
water.

4 酢水を捨て、水でしっかりとすす
ぐ。

Discard the liquid and rinse the ohitsu
thoroughly with water.

2 桶いっぱいに水を張り、酢大さじ4
くらいを入れる。

Fill the ohitsu with water and add
about four tablespoons of vinegar.

5 布巾で水気を拭く。

Wipe dry with a cloth.

3 1〜2時間おくと、木の独特なにおい
がやわらぎ、汚れがつきにくくなる。

Leave for one to two hours. This
reduces the new wood smell and makes
the surface more resistant to grease and
stains.

6 拭いた後でもすぐにしまわずに、ひ
と晩くらいおいてしっかりと乾かす。

Do not put the ohitsu away
immediately after wiping. Leave out at
least overnight to dry completely.

木・竹の道具 ……… 桶細工のおひつ

日々の手入れ Daily care

1 使用後はそのまま放置せず、なるべく早く水かぬるま湯で洗う。

Do not leave the ohitsu unwashed after use. Wash with water or lukewarm water as soon as possible.

2 1で汚れが落ちない場合は、タワシかスポンジを使って洗う。中性洗剤やクレンザーを使ってもいい。

If it is not clean enough, wash with a tawashi, a scrubbing brush or a sponge. A mild detergent or a powder cleanser can be used.

困ったときは Troubleshooting

黒ズミが発生したとき
Darkening

かまぼこ板くらいの大きさの板に、目の細かいサンドペーパー（＃200程度）を巻き、黒ズミ部分に平行にあててこする。

Wrap a piece of fine sandpaper (about #200) around a small wooden block. Place the block parallel to the darkened area and sand.

ヤニが気になるとき
Resin

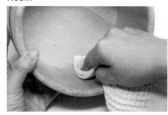

濡れたような濃い色になるのは椹のヤニ（樹脂）。布などに消毒用アルコールを染み込ませて拭けば取れる。

A dark and wet looking color is caused by resin from Sawara cypress. It can be removed by wiping with a cloth soaked in an alcohol-based disinfectant.

やってはいけないこと
DON'TS

電子レンジ Microwave	食洗機 Dishwasher	金属タワシ Metallic scrubber	天日干し Dry in direct sunlight

冷蔵庫 Keep in the refrigerator

滴生舎の

漆の器

Urushi Lacquerware / Tekiseisha

浄漆椀 中・大　Joshitsuwan (Urushi Bowls) medium, large

素材 Materials	ミズメ、栃、漆 Mizume (Japanese cherry birch), tochinoki (Japanese horse-chestnut), urushi (Japanese lacquer)
サイズ Dimensions	中:直径12.8×高さ6.9cm　大:直径13.6×高さ8.5cm M: D12.8 x H6.9cm　L: D13.6 x H8.5cm
主な取扱い店 Stockists	滴生舎 松屋銀座デザインコレクション d47 design travel store Tekiseisha Matsuya Ginza Design Collection d47 design travel store

その他のラインナップ Product Information

浄漆椀は小サイズもある。ほかに角椀、ねそり（コップ）、弁当箱（丸と角）など。すべて朱色と溜色がある。

The joshitsuwan urushi bowl is also available in small size. Other products available include faceted bowls, nesori cups, bento lunch boxes (round and square) and come in shu-iro (vermillion) and tame-iro (blackish brown).

漆器は漆の木の樹液を木地に塗ることで、器として成り立つ。「漆掻き」という職人が漆の木を専用の刃物で傷つけると、漆の木は傷を保護するため樹液を出す。いわば、かさぶたのようなものだ。漆は一本の木から牛乳瓶一本程度しか採れないが、この貴重な樹液は、器の土台となる木地を丈夫にさせるだけでなく、独特の艶とふっくらとした質感を生み出す。

漆は軽く、そして熱をやわらげる。器を手に持って食事をすることが多い和食に合った素材といえるのだ。

一度使いだすと、こんなに良いものはないと思うのが漆。軽い、質感が良い、使い込んだ味わいが出る、割れにくい（ただし、落とせばヒビは入る）、そして、意外なことに扱いが楽。私の場合は、ぬるま湯と布のスポンジで洗って終わり。洗剤は使わない。落とさない、熱湯（100度以上）を入れない程度の気の使い方だから、要はガラスと一緒だと思えばいい。滴生舎で塗師（漆を塗る人）の小田島勇さんに手入れ法を聞いても「使うのが一番」と、手入れより使うことをすすめられる。日常的に使って洗うこと。たまにしか使わないのが、一番悪い手入れなのだ。

落として欠けたり、熱湯を入れて白濁してしまったものでも、塗り直しはできる。ただし、塗り直しは、一度塗った漆を剥がしてから塗り直すため、新品同様になる。つまり、使い込んだ艶や風合いはなくなってしまうのだ。

Shikki or Japanese urushi lacquerware is made by applying urushi sap to the body of a wooden vessel. When urushikaki, a tapper who specializes in collecting sap from urushi trees, puts scars on the bark, the tree produces sap to protect the wound and it quickly hardens like a scab on cut skin. The sap extracted from a single urushi tree may be as little as 200ml. This precious liquid not only makes the base wood more durable but creates a soft, warm texture and exquisite luster.

The urushi ware is light and heat-resistant and this makes it ideal for Japanese-style meals, because vessels are often held in hands while eating.

The more you use the urushi ware, the more you will realize how good it is for every-day use. It is light, nice to touch and the texture improves with use. It does not crack easily (but it can crack if dropped) and is surprisingly easy to look after. I wash my urushi ware using only lukewarm water and a dish sponge made of cotton, without detergent. It is almost the same as handling glassware; be mindful not to drop it or not to pour anything boiling hot in it. I asked Isamu Odashima, who works as lacquering artisan at Tekiseisha, for advice on how to care for urushi ware. He recommended, "Just use it and that is the best for urushi," instead of worrying about maintenance. Use it every day and wash. Using only occasionally is the poorest way to care for your urushi ware. If your urushi ware has been chipped or turned cloudy white with hot water, it can be repaired by stripping the old coatings and reapplying new. It will look as good as brand-new but, at all the same time, the luster and rich texture that has developed over use will be lost.

木・竹の道具 …… 漆の器

日々の手入れ Daily care

1 使用後、油が気にならない場合は、
水かぬるま湯で流して洗えばOK。

If the bowl is not too greasy after use,
just wash with water or lukewarm
water.

2 油が気になる場合は、スポンジに
中性洗剤をつけて洗う。

If the bowl is greasy, wash with a mild
detergent and a sponge.

3 水かぬるま湯ですすいだら、布巾
で拭いて水気を取る。

After rinsing the bowl with water or
lukewarm water, wipe dry with a cloth.

4 拭いた後もすぐにはしまわないで、
ひと晩ほど置いて乾かしておく。

Do not put the bowl away immediately
after wiping. Leave out to dry at least
overnight.

5 完全に乾いたら、直射日光の当た
らないところにしまう。

When the bowl is completely dry, store
it in a place with no direct sunlight.

やってはいけないこと
DON'TS

電子レンジ Microwave	食洗機 Dishwasher	金属タワシ Metallic scrubber	天日干し Dry in direct sunlight
冷蔵庫 Keep in the refrigerator			

漆の手入れの良い例と悪い例
Example of good and poor care

下が新品の器で、上に重なっているのが5年ほど使った器。ほとんど毎日使い、左ページのとおりの手入れをしているだけなのに、美しい艶が出て、新品のものと確実に異なる風合いになっている。洗剤を使わないほうが艶は出る。

The bowl at bottom is brand new. The one on top is about five years old and used almost every day. Just with the basic care shown on the previous page it has developed a beautiful gloss and more texture, which the new bowl has not. The glossiness increases by washing without any detergent.

椀の内部にヒビが入ってしまった。これは極度の乾燥により木地が縮み、漆が浮いたために生じた悪い例。

Extremely dry condition has caused shrinkage of the wood and peeling of the lacquer, which has resulted in a crack inside the bowl.

椀の上部2/3ほどが白く濁ったように変色している。これは直射日光が当たるところに、重ねて置いていたために起きてしまった悪い例。

The color of the upper 2/3 of the bowl has turned cloudy white. This is an example of poor care. Discoloration has been caused by stacking the bowls inside each other and leaving exposed to direct sunlight.

椀提供／滴生舎

39

漆の器の作り手を訪ねる

滴生舎

Visiting Tekiseisha / Maker of urushi lacquerware

　岩手県二戸市浄法寺は漆の樹液の産地。1995年に全国でも珍しい、市営の漆器製造併設の販売所「滴生舎」がオープンした。

　漆の作業はいたって地味だ。浄法寺の技法は、塗っては研ぎ、塗っては研ぐの繰り返し。高価な漆を研ぐのは、次の漆の食いつきを良くするためだ。そして7層にもなった漆器は、厚さ1mmにも満たないが、ふっくらとした質感に仕上がる。

　滴生舎の塗師、小田島勇さんがデザインした浄漆椀は、「上質」に掛けたただのじゃれだが、本当に上質椀といっていい贅沢をしている。通常は国産価格の約1/10の中国産漆を使うのに、下地も国産を使用。値段の違いは主に人件費の違いだが、国産の方が延びが良く、できれば国産を使いたい、と思う作り手がほとんどだ。塗ってもほとんど研いでしまう下地は、何を塗っても良さそうなものだが、この椀の豊かな艶やかさは、やはり下地がものをいっているのかもしれない。

Joboji in Ninohe City, Iwate Prefecture, is a leading production area of urushi (Japanese lacquer) sap. Tekiseisha was opened 1995. Tekiseisha is a city-run urusi lacquerware manufacturing facility and store, a quite rare business model in Japan.

Lacquering is monotonous work. The Joboji method requires a repeated "sanding and lacquering" process. At Tekiseisha they use expensive urushi sap to provide better adhesion for the next layer. The finished products have seven layers, and though less than 1mm thick, these layers of lacquer give the urushi ware a soft and full texture.

"Joshitsuwan", Tekiseisha's original urushi bowls were designed by Isamu Odashima, nuri-shi (lacquering artisan) at Tekiseisha. The name "Joshitsuwan" is a short form of Joboji's shitsuwan (urushi bowls). It is also a pun using homonym because "Joshitsu" also means high quality in Japanese, and their use of high quality urushi confirms it. While urushi makers these days use imported urushi from China, which is about one tenth of the cost of the local Japanese product, Tekiseisha uses local urushi for undercoats as well as for finishing coat. The gap in the urushi prices is mainly due to labor cost but Japanese urushi is superior in quality and most makers would prefer to use it if they could afford. Most urushi applied for undercoating is sanded off, so its quality may seem insignificant, but the secret of the exquisite luster of their urushi bowls may well lie in those thin invisible layers underneath.

1.滴生舎は下地も日本産を使っている。地元ならではの贅沢だ。2.「研いでは塗る」を繰り返すのが漆。ろくろを使い、効率良く研ぐ。3.漆は、それぞれ色だけでなく乾き具合も違う。

1.At Tekiseisha, they use Japanese urushi for undercoating as well. It is an expensive practice that only local producers can afford. 2.Urushi work requires repeated "sanding and lacquering". The sanding is carried out efficiently on a pottery wheel. 3.Each urushi is a different color and the drying time also varies.

1.椀はろくろで研ぐが、さじは一本ずつ手で研ぐ地道な作業だ。さじは力が入りやすいので、椀より耐久性を求められる。2.漆が固まるには温度と湿度が必要。「漆風呂」と呼ばれる専用の場所に置き、塗るたびに硬化させる。3.漆の樹液を保存するための樽。この樽も岩手で作られている。

1.Bowls are sanded on a pottery wheel but spoons are hand-sanded one by one. It is painstaking work. Spoons need to be more durable than bowls to hold weight. 2.For urushi to become solid, a certain level of temperature and humidity is required. Urushi bowls are kept in an "urushi-buro" (urushi bath) to harden after each coating. 3.Wooden barrels for storing urushi sap. They are also made locally in Iwate.

作り手の使い方

滴生舎で働く人のお昼は、それぞれが持参した弁当。その2段の弁当箱は、滴生舎に入舎したときにもらったものだ。蓋は味噌汁椀として使う。電気ポットからお湯を入れてインスタントの味噌汁を作るが、ポットだと75度以下だから、漆も大丈夫。

How the makers use it

At Tekiseisha employees bring their own bento lunch. They receive this two-tier lunch box at the beginning of their employment. The lid is used as a soup bowl. They use hot water from an electric pot to make instant soup and the water temperature is lower than 75 degrees, so it is safe for urushi ware.

喜八工房の

拭き漆の器

Fuki-urushi Lacquerware / *Kihachi Kobo*

栓 三つ組の器 拭き漆　Sen　Set of Three Fuki-urushi Nestling Bowls

素材 Materials	栓、漆 Sen wood (castor aralia), urushi
サイズ Dimensions	小:直径10×高さ4.2cm　中:直径11×高さ5.6cm 大:直径12×高さ7cm S: D10 x H4.2cm　M: D11 x H5.6cm　L: D12 x H7cm
主な取扱い店	喜八工房 金沢ひがし茶屋街漆器直売処(喜八工房 金沢東山店) J-PERIOD BALS TOKYO
Stockists	Kihachi Kobo Kanazawa Higashichayagai Shikki Chokubaijo (Kihachi Kobo Kanazawa Higashiyama Store) J-PERIOD BALS TOKYO

その他のラインナップ
Product Information

拭き漆には糸筋椀、フリーボウル、汁椀などのアイテムがある。赤(朱)、黒、溜の漆のアイテムも数多く揃う。

Other fuki-urushi items available include Itosuji bowls, all purpose bowls and soup bowls. Many urushi products are also available in shu (vermillion), black and tame (blackish brown).

漆を「塗っては拭き」を繰り返して作るのが拭き漆。手間が少なく、漆を乾かす（硬化させる）時間も短いので、短期間で作れ、価格も比較的安価だ。拭き漆は、木の木目を引き立たせるために漆が塗られる。拭いているとはいえ、漆は5回ほど塗り重ね、木目を浮き上がらせていくのだ。

　拭き漆は、傷が見えにくいので、多少手荒に扱っても大丈夫なように感じる。ただし、漆が薄いため、素地が出やすい。口をつける縁、底といった摩擦の多い部分は漆が剝げやすい。木肌が見えた状態で使い続けると、木の中に水が浸透し、木を傷めることになるので早めに直しに出すべきだ。

Fuki-urushi ware is made by a repeated process of applying urushi to the wooden base and wiping off the excess. Because of its straightforward method and less drying or hardening time, the production time for fuki-urushi ware is reasonably short and the price is affordable. For the fuki-urushi, lacquer is used to highlight the wood grain. Although the focus of the process is on wiping the lacquer it is applied at least five times to make the grain more prominent.

The fuki-urushi seems to endure rough handling because scratch marks are not so visible, but the thin coating means the bare wood tends to be exposed after many uses. The coating wears off more on the rim where the user's lips touch and the bottom that has direct contact with surfaces. If the bare wood is left exposed, water seeps into the wood and eventually damages it, so early repair is recommended.

日々の手入れ Daily care

1 食べ残しが付着している場合は無理にこすらず、5分ほど水に浸けてふやかしておく。

If there is any left-over food stuck on the bowl, do not use force to remove. Soak the bowl in water for about five minutes to soften the food.

2 中性洗剤をつけて手で洗うのがおすすめだが。柔らかいスポンジを使ってもOK。

Hand washing with a mild detergent is recommended but a sponge can also be used.

やってはいけないこと
DON'TS

| 電子レンジ Microwave | 食洗機 Dishwasher | 金属タワシ Metallic scrubber | 天日干し Dry in direct sunlight |

| 冷蔵庫 Keep in the refrigerator |

久保一幸の

竹の籠

Bamboo Basket / Kazuyuki Kubo

波ござ目籠 小　Namigozame Kago Basket small

素材 Materials	真竹、籐 Madake bamboo (Japanese timber bamboo), rattan
サイズ Dimensions	21.5×16.5×高さ5.5cm 21.5 x 16.5 x H5.5cm
主な取扱い店	LIVINGMOTIF 秋篠の森 月草
Stockists	LIVINGMOTIF Akishino no Mori Tsukikusa

その他のラインナップ Product Information

波ござ目籠は中サイズもある。ほかに、片口籠、竹飯籠、亀甲編み長皿、そば笊、竹のバッグなど多数のアイテムがある。

The namigozame kago basket also comes in medium size. Many other items are available including lipped baskets, bamboo rice containers, tortoise-shell weave long plates, soba zaru (serving sieves for soba noodles) and bamboo bags.

竹の大きな特徴は節があり、そしてしなること。それゆえ、籠制作に向き、そのすがすがしい趣で食卓にも合う。竹籠は素材の加工の仕方と竹の種類によって何種類もある。

久保一幸さんは真竹を使う。節と節の間が長いので、作業がしやすいからだ。伐採後、苛性ソーダを混ぜた水で煮て、竹の中の油分を落とす。油抜きをすることで緑からクリーム色になり、その色と質感が持続する。久保さんが通った竹工芸の職業訓練校では基本的な編み方を数パターン学び、卒業後、多くの人がその延長線上での技法を使ってもの作りをする。作者が違っても見た目が似た籠が多いのはそのためだ。久保さんは基本を大切にしながら、独自にアレンジした籠を作り、海外の人にもファンが多い。ちょっと気を使って扱ってもらいたいと、必要以上に丁寧に面取りしたヒゴで、繊細なものを編む。

竹の籠は編んであることを意識して使うのがポイント。交差しているところに水分が残っているとカビの元になるので、きちんと乾かすこと。乾きにくさを考えると、水に長いこと浸すのは好ましくない。竹は表皮が堅いので丈夫ではあるが、油は浸透する。油ものを盛るときは、紙などを敷いてシミを防ぐが、シミができても、使い込むうちになじんでいくので問題ない。

Bamboo's distinctive characteristics are its nodes and supple stems. The flexibility of bamboo makes it an ideal material for basketry and a bamboo basket adds a fresh, soothing look to any dining table. There are various types of bamboo and processing methods to make bamboo baskets.

Kazuyuki Kubo uses madake (Japanese timber bamboo) because it has long stems that are easy to work on. After being cut down, the bamboo trees are boiled in caustic soda water to remove excess oil. This process changes the color of the bamboo from green to creamy white and makes the color and texture last longer. At the training center Kazuyuki attended, the students learn basic weaving techniques for several patterns. Many graduates continue to apply these techniques to make their own pieces and this is why bamboo baskets made by different craftsmen tend to look similar. While respecting the basics, Kazuyuki makes bamboo baskets with a twist and has many admirers overseas as well as in Japan. He takes the extra trouble to smooth out bamboo sticks to create a delicately woven basket and hopes that the users will also give a little extra attention to his creations.

When handling a bamboo basket, we should keep in mind that it is made of interlaced strips. The overlapping areas need to be dried well, otherwise any leftover moisture can cause mold. For the same reason it is not recommended to soak a bamboo basket in water for a long period of time. Although bamboo is durable with a tough outer skin, oil can seep in. You can line the basket with a paper towel for stain-proofing before placing oily foods. Oil stains are however not too big a concern. They will eventually blend into the bamboo with use.

木・竹の道具
……
竹の籠

日々の手入れ Daily care

1 使用後は、タワシに中性洗剤をつけ、編み目に沿って洗う。

After use, wash the basket along the weaving patterns using a mild detergent and a tawashi or a scrubbing brush.

2 タワシで軽くこすりながら、水かぬるま湯で洗剤をすすぐ。

Rinse off the detergent with water or lukewarm water while rubbing gently with a tawashi or a scrubbing brush.

3 布巾で拭いて水気を取る。

Wipe the basket with a cloth to dry.

4 布巾で拭いただけでは乾かないため、すぐにしまわないで立て掛けて乾かしておく。

Do not put the basket away immediately after wiping. Prop it up and leave to air dry so that it is completely dry.

5 できるだけ密閉したところにしまいこまない。空気の流れる場所に立て掛けて置くのが好ましい。

Avoid storing the bamboo basket in a closed place. It is recommended to stand it on one end and keep in a well-ventilated place.

注意すること Special attention

天ぷらなどの油を使った料理をのせるときは、クッキングシートなどを1枚敷く。

Before placing deep-fried food such as tempura in the basket, line the inside with a baking paper.

油揚げの油抜きに使うと、油がついた部分だけ色が変わってくる。何度も行うといい具合に色がなじんでくるが、色の変化が気になる人は避けたほうがいい。

If the basket is used for parboiling deep-fried tofu to remove excess oil, the color in oiled area of the basket will change. It will blend in when the process is repeated, but if you prefer not to have this color change, then do not use the basket for this purpose.

使っているうちに竹が途中で切れ、飛び出してしまう場合も。手にささらないように気をつけて扱う。

Bamboo strips can get broken with use and stick out. The splints can prick your hand, so handle carefully.

困ったときは Troubleshooting

カビたとき
Mold

カビた部分にクレンザーをふりかけ、歯ブラシでこすり、水で洗い流す。

Sprinkle a powder cleanser on the moldy area. Rub with a toothbrush and rinse with water.

やってはいけないこと
DON'TS

 電子レンジ Microwave
 食洗機 Dishwasher
 金属タワシ Metallic scrubber
 天日干し Dry in direct sunlight

竹の籠の作り手を訪ねる

久保一幸さん

Visiting Kazuyuki Kubo / Maker of bamboo baskets

日本で一番の竹籠の産地は大分県。全国で唯一の竹の訓練支援センターがあり、多くの職人を輩出している。久保一幸さんはもともと理系で、電子部品のメーカーに勤めていたが、ひとりでできる技術を身につけようと、この訓練校に入学した。

竹籠の醍醐味は編むことと思われがちだが、最も重要なのは下準備。竹を割り、ヒゴを作る丁寧さが、作品となったとき、その差に歴然と現れる。竹は、おおらかな作業に見えるが、同じものを正確に作り続けるためには、図面を書き、ヒゴの細さや長さも㎜単位で書き入れていく。しかし、作業は素人目には目分量でやっているように見えてしまう。一見、大雑把に見える刃物の調整も、「先達から受け継がれた技でしっかり留めておけば、何百回の作業でも同じ幅になる」と言う。さらにヒゴは2枚に梳く。この2枚剥ぎが、籠のしなやかさを醸し出すことになる。

久保さんの作る籠は、独特のかたちが多い。基本が限られているので、アレンジが難しい技法ながら、これだけのかたちを生み出すのは珍しいのだ。

Oita Prefecture is the largest production center of the bamboo baskets in Japan and has a training support center for bamboo crafts. The center is the only one in the whole country and has produced many bamboo craftsmen. Kazuyuki Kubo was a science student and worked for a company making electronic parts. Later Kazuyuki wanted to acquire skills to work for himself and enrolled in the training center. While weaving is thought to be the most enjoyable part of bamboo work, preparation is the most important part of the process. Paying close attention to the groundwork such as splitting bamboo and making sticks makes a huge difference to the outcome.

Although bamboo work seems uncomplicated, it involves a draft drawing and writing in the thickness and the length of bamboo sticks on the millimeter to make uniform-sized products. To inexperienced eyes, craftsmen seem to be making measurements by guessing and adjusting their cutting tools without paying much attention. But they say, "As long as we attach the blades to the base securely using the techniques passed down from our senior craftsmen, we can make several hundred sticks with the same width." Already thin bamboo sticks are split into two and this process brings out the elasticity of bamboo.

Kazuyuki's baskets have unique shapes. As the basic techniques and patterns are rather limited, bamboo work is not an easy craft in which to make variations. Kazuyuki has the rare talent to come up with such creative shapes and ideas.

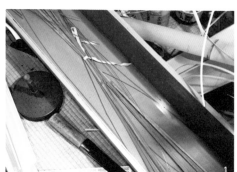

1.ヒゴにした竹は水で湿らせて柔らかくしてから編む。2.ヒゴの幅取り。このひと手間が仕上げに関わってくる。

1.The bamboo sticks are soaked in water to soften before weaving. 2.The habatori process to make each stick an even width. This extra work makes a difference in the finishing process.

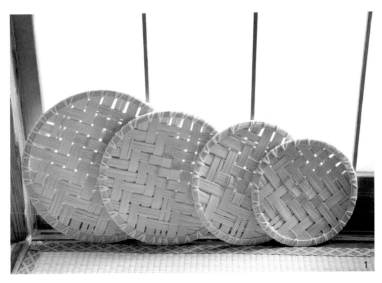

1.「そば笊」。新しいものを作るときは、試作を繰り返し、使い心地を試す。大胆に割った竹を数本ずつまとめて編む、ダイナミックなざるだ。2.作品として作ったもの。雑器の扱いではなく、乾きものを入れて、拭きながらきれいに保ちたい美しさだ。3.お店の要望で作った緻密な編みのプレートカバー。

1."Soba zaru" (bamboo sieve for serving soba noodles). When creating a new design, Kazuyuki makes many prototypes and tests them out by himself. These baskets are made by weaving several wide strips together, creating bold patterns. 2.This basket was made for exhibition. A beautiful piece like this should only be used for holding dry snacks and its quality maintained through good care. 3.This delicately woven plate cover is a made-to-order piece requested by a shop owner.

作り手の使い方

1.「片口」というお題の元に作った籠。日本酒の2合瓶を入れてもしゃれているが、リンゴなどのフルーツを入れてもさまになる。
2.六角の弁当箱。おむすびがきれいに収まる。ぶつけやすい角は、6カ所とも籐でしっかりガードしている。

How the makers use it

1.The basket was made on the theme of "katakuchi" (lipped). It would make a stylish container for a small Japanese sake bottle but also looks pretty when containing fruit like apples. 2.Rice balls fit nicely in this hexagonal bento basket. Each corner of the basket is enforced with rattan to protect against bumping.

田代淳さんに教わる
金継ぎ教室

**Jun Tashiro's
Kintsugi Workshop**

「金継ぎ」とは、欠けたり割れたりした陶磁器を漆で継ぎ、金や銀の粉を蒔き、上化粧して直すこと。茶の湯が盛んだった室町時代に、茶道の世界ではじまったといわれている。漆は椀などの木の器に塗るものと思っている人も多いだろうが、接着剤にもなるのだから、おもしろい素材なのだ。

　金継ぎは、器の壊れた状態によってその方法は異なる。ここでは、小さな欠けが生じた場合と、完全に割れてしまった場合の金継ぎの方法を、漆作家で金継ぎも行う田代淳さんに教えてもらった。「最近は金継ぎに必要な道具がセットになったものがホームセンターなどでも手に入り、金継ぎが身近になったように思います。金継ぎはそんなに難しいことではありませんが、漆の練り方などにちょっとしたコツが必要です。自分ではじめられる前に、体験教室などに参加することをおすすめします。プロのやり方を間近で見ると、コツがしっかりつかめるはずです」と田代さん。

　修復された器は、元の姿とはまた違う、新しい表情を見せてくれる。それを自分の手で蘇らせたとなれば、より愛着がわき、大切にすることになるに違いない。

"Kintsugi" ("to patch with urushi" in Japanese) is a repair method to restore broken ceramics. It uses urushi lacquer to join chipped or broken pieces of vessels and fine gold or silver powder to burnish. Kintsugi is said to have originated in the Muromachi period (1338-1573) through the flourishing practice of chanoyu (Japanese tea ceremony). Urushi is widely known as lacquer paint for wooden vessels, but it also makes a strong adhesive. It is certainly an interesting material to work with.

The kintsugi method varies depending on how the vessel is damaged. Jun Tashiro, urushi artist and kintsugi practitioner, shows how to repair a small chip and broken pieces. "Because kintsugi repair kits are readily available at hardware stores, these days more people are getting to know about it. Kintsugi is not hard to do but you need to have a bit of skill, like mixing raw urushi and water properly. I recommend anyone who wants to try kintsugi at home to join a one-day class first. You can learn a few tricks by closely watching the way a professional works," says Jun.

The restored piece has a fresh look, different from the original, and when you have done the repair by yourself you will feel more attached to the piece and treasure it for a long time.

田代さんが金継ぎした器
Vessels restored by Jun Tashiro

1.3つに割れた部分に金継ぎをした小島鉄平さん作の豆皿。2.生漆のみで継いだ骨董の湯呑み。3.田代さんごひいきの、盛岡のカフェ「carta」で使用している安藤雅信さん作のプレート。田代さんが生漆で継いだ。4.鈴木稔さん作のカップの縁の部分の欠けを金継ぎした。

1.Mamezara (tiny plate) by ceramic artist Teppei Kojima. The three broken pieces were joined with kintsugi. 2.Antique tea cup was restored only with raw urushi. 3.Plate by ceramic artist Masanobu Ando is used at "carta", Jun's favorite café in Morioka City. Jun used raw urushi to repair the plate. 4.Small cup by ceramic artist Minoru Suzuki. The chipped rim was restored with kintsugi.

田代淳さん　Jun Tashiro
岩手県安代町漆器センターで2年間漆器作りを学ぶ。2010年から盛岡市に住み、漆器作家として活動しながら、金継ぎも行う。全国各地で金継ぎのワークショップも実施している。http://jun-tashi.com

Jun Tashiro studied urushi ware artistry for two years at Iwate Ashirocho Shikki Center and has been living in Morioka City in Iwate Prefecture since 2010. While working as urushiware artist, Jun also practices kintsugi and teaches kintsugi classes at various workshops throughout Japan.

金継ぎに必要な
主な材料と道具
Materials and Tools

①テレビン：そうじ用に使う溶剤。②砥の粉：錆を作る材料。③へら：漆を混ぜて練り合わせるのに使う。④サンドペーパー：錆で埋めた部分を滑らかにする。⑤ガラス板：パテや漆を練り合わせる台として使う。⑥金粉：漆で補修した部分に化粧として蒔く。⑦アートナイフ：乾いた錆を削り、器の元のかたちになるように成形するのに使う。⑧細い筆：漆を塗るのに使う。⑨生漆：チューブ入りが便利。
※ほかにダイヤモンドの棒ヤスリや真綿、セロテープなども必要。
※金継ぎのキットはホームセンターや漆屋さんのネットショップなどで買える。

①Turpentine: cleaning solvent ②Tonoko mixing medium: for making sabi paste ③Spatula: for mixing urushi ④Sandpaper: for polishing ⑤Glass sheet: for mixing putty or urushi ⑥Gold power ⑦Art knife: for scraping dried sabi paste to bring a broken vessel back to its original shape ⑧Fine brush: for applying urushi ⑨Raw urushi: A tube raw urushi is easy to use
※ Other items required for kintsugi include a diamond coated file, mawata (floss silk) and sticky tape or masking tape.
※ Kintsugi repair kits are available at hardware stores and urushi maker's online shops.

金継ぎのおおまかな流れ Kintsugi Process

小さく欠けた場合
Chipped piece

1

欠けは生漆に砥の粉を混ぜた「錆」というパテで埋める。まずは砥の粉を水で練る。

The chipped part is to be filled in with putty called "sabi", a mixture of urushi and tonoko powder. To begin, mix tonoko with water.

2

1に生漆を混ぜて練って錆を作る。

Mix urushi with the tonoko paste to make "sabi".

3

欠けた部分に、2の錆を薄くつけ、乾いたらまたつけるを器の元の輪郭になるまで繰り返す。

Apply a thin layer of "sabi" to the chipped part and let it dry. Repeat the process until the chipped part is filled in.

※漆は素手でふれると、かぶれる可能性があります。田代さんは慣れているので素手ですが、必ず手袋をして作業しましょう。

※Urushi can cause rash when handled with bare hands. Jun works with bare hands because she is experienced, but make sure you wear gloves when handing urushi.

56

割れた場合
Broken pieces

割れは練った小麦粉と生漆を混ぜて作る「麦漆」で接着させる。まずは割れた箇所のエッジの部分をダイヤモンドの棒ヤスリでさっと削る。

Broken pieces are to be bonded together with "mugi-urushi" paste made by mixing flour and urushi. To begin, give the broken edges a quick sanding with a diamond-coated file.

小麦粉に水を加え、耳たぶくらいの柔らかさになるまで練る。

Add water to flour and mix until the mixture has the consistency of earlobe.

2に生漆を混ぜて麦漆を作る。へらで持ち上げて写真のような粘りが出たらOK。

Add urushi to the mixture to make mugi-urushi paste. When it has stringy consistency when lifted as shown in the photograph, it is done.

割れた断面に3の麦漆を塗る。

Apply the mugi-urushi paste to the broken edges.

割れたもの同士をくっつける。

Take another broken piece to bond with the first.

麦漆がはみ出たところはへらで取り除く（釉薬によっては漆が染みる可能性があるので注意）。

Use spatula to take excess paste off (Please note that some glazes allow urushi to seep into ceramics).

麦漆は動かない程度に乾くまで時間がかかるため、接着した部分にセロテープを貼って固定する。その後、溝を錆で埋める。

Mugi-urushi takes some time to dry. Put sticky tape or masking tape on the bonded areas to hold in place. Later fill in any holes with sabi putty.

仕上げに金粉を蒔くとき
How to apply the finishing gold powder

小さく欠けた場合と割れた場合のそれぞれの工程を終えたら、錆の上に漆を数回塗る。仕上げに金粉（または銀粉。ともにパウダー状の消粉の場合）を蒔く場合は漆を塗り、乾きかけのタイミングで金粉を蒔く。

When the bonding process is completed, apply urushi to the sabi several times. If you are using gold powder (or silver powder, and the finest type, keshifun), apply urushi first and dust the powder before the urushi is completely dried.

細い筆で漆を塗り、漆が乾く少し前に、真綿を使って金粉を蒔きつける。

Apply urushi with a fine brush. Before the urushi is completely dried, use mawata to dab gold powder on the joints.

土の道具

Earthen Utensils

食卓に並ぶ器の多くは陶磁器だろう。
粘土を高温で焼いてできあがるが、素材は大きく2つに分かれる。
石を粉砕した陶石を使い、硬質で、叩くと金属音に近い音がする磁器。
そして、陶土という土が原料で、柔らかみがあり、
指ではじくと鈍い音がする陶器。
水を吸わない磁器には特別な手入れが不要なため、
この章では、水を吸うという特性から、
シミができることもある陶器類の手入れを紹介する。

Most common tableware used at home is probably ceramics: pottery
and porcelain. Both are made by baking clay at high temperatures but
they use different materials. Porcelain consists of ceramic stone. It is
hard and makes a metallic sound when flicked with fingers. Pottery is
made from potter's clay. It has a touch of warm softness and makes a
dull sound when flicked. Porcelain is non-porous and does not require
special care. Pottery on the other hand absorbs water and therefore is
prone to stains. In this chapter, I will explain how to care for pottery
vessels.

粉引・白マットの器

Kohiki and Matte White Ware / Mikiko Iyama

猿山プレート（粉引） Saruyama Plate (kohiki)
面取りマグカップ（白マット） Faceted Mug (matte white)

素材 Materials	プレート：陶器、マグ：半磁器 Plate: Pottery, Mug: Semi-porcelain
サイズ Dimensions	プレート：13.3×9.2×高さ1.8㎝ マグ：直径7×高さ7.5㎝ Plate: 13.3 x 9.2 x H1.8cm Mug: D7 x H7.5cm
主な取扱い店 Stockists	KOHORO Zakka 木と根 くるみの木cage KOHORO Zakka Kitone Kuruminoki cage

その他のラインナップ Product Information

粉引と白マット、黒マットが中心。陶器、半磁器以外に、耐火土で、目玉焼きパンや鍋などもある。

Items available are mainly kohiki, matte white and matte black ware.
Besides pottery and semi-porcelain, heat-resistant clay items such as egg
frying pans and cooking pots are also available.

白と黒の器を作る井山三希子さん。白は2タイプを制作する。粉引と白マットだ。粉引の素地は陶土で、陶器である。粉引は陶土の上に白い化粧土をかけるが、一般的には水をよく吸い込むので、ガラス質になる釉薬をかけて仕上げる。一方、白マットの土は、陶土に陶石を調合した半磁器だが、陶器の分類になるので、焼き上げてから艶のない白の釉薬をかける。粉引のほうが土台の赤土の色が透けてやや赤めに仕上がり、白マットのほうが水の浸透がやや遅く、「貫入」が入りにくいという違いがある。

貫入とは、素地に細かくヒビ状に色がついてくること。作り方や焼き方によって、入りやすいものと入りにくいものがある。貫入を防ぐため、陶器の使いはじめには、米のとぎ汁で煮るようにと言われた人も多いはず。これは賛成派と反対派に分かれる。米のとぎ汁で煮ても、貫入は入る。反対派としては、米のとぎ汁はカビを誘発するので、料理や飲み物を入れる前に毎回、水に浸してから使うことをすすめている。井山さんは水浸透派だ。

貫入のおもしろさは、同じ作者のものですら同じニュアンスにならないので、自分だけの味わいに育てていけること。粉引と白マットの器には、貫入を楽しむおおらかさが必要なのだ。

Mikiko Iyama uses two colors for her ceramic works: black and white. With white, she makes two types of pottery vessels: kohiki and matte white. Kohiki is pottery made from potter's clay, which absorbs water. A vessel is dipped in white slip first and glazed to become vitrified. Although it is called semi-porcelain, matte white is also a type of pottery made from mixed materials of clay and clay stone. Non-gloss white glaze is applied to the vessel after baking in a kilm. Kohiki pottery has reddish finish with the color of its body showing through. Matte white pottery is more resistant to water penetration and this makes it less prone to "kan-nyuu".

Kan-nyuu is fine, colored crackle on the body of a pottery vessel that becomes visible over use. How kan-nyuu forms largely depends on how each piece of pottery was made and fired. Many readers might have been advised to boil their pottery in togijiru (milky water left after rinsing uncooked rice) before the first use. There are conflicting opinions about this method. In fact, boiling pottery in togijiru does not necessarily stop kan-nyuu and togijiru can cause mold. As someone who is opposed to the boiling method, I would recommend a soaking method instead; submerging the pottery before placing foods or pouring drinks. Mikiko also supports the soaking method.

A fascinating aspect of kan-nyuu is that it brings a fine nuance in each piece pf pottery even though it is made by the same artisan. The owner of the pottery can enjoy seeing his or her piece develop a character of its own over time. It requires relaxed approach to fully appreciate the uniqueness of kan-nyuu in kohiki and matte white ware.

日々の手入れ Daily care

使う前
Before use

1 油や食べ物の色がつくのを防ぐため、料理を盛る前に水に浸す。

Before placing food, soak the plate in water to prevent oil and food stains.

2 器が水を吸っている証拠に泡が出てくる。全体の色が変わったら（浸水後2～5分）取り出して、布巾で軽く拭く。

When the plate absorbs water, air bubbles start to appear. When the color of the plate has changed (after about 2-5 minutes of soaking), take it out of the water and wipe dry with a cloth.

やってはいけないこと
DON'TS

| 電子レンジ Microwave | 食洗機 Dishwasher | 金属タワシ Metallic scrubber |

使った後
After use

1 使用後は、スポンジに中性洗剤をつけて洗う。

Wash the plate with a mild detergent and a sponge.

2 水かぬるま湯で洗剤をすすぐ。

Rinse with water or lukewarm water.

3 布巾で拭いたら、しっかり乾かしておく。すぐにしまわず、ひと晩ほど乾かしてからしまう。

Dry thoroughly after wiping with a cloth. Leave out to dry at least overnight before storing.

粉引と白マットの違いと貫入の入り方

The difference between kohiki (left) and matte white (right) and
how kan-nyuu forms.

写真左が粉引で右が白マットの器。見分けがつきにくいこともある器だが、こうして裏返してみると
一目瞭然。粉引は赤土で作っているため、白い化粧土の掛かっていない部分に赤土が見える。

At first glance it is hard to tell them apart, but the difference is quite clear once they are turned over.
The red clay in kohiki shows at the back of the plate where no white slip (engobe) has been applied.

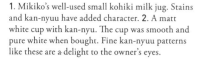

1.井山さんが使い込んでいる粉引のピッチャー。シ
ミと貫入の入り方がいい味わいとなっている。2.白
マットに貫入が入ったもの。もちろん、はじめは貫
入がまったく入っていない真っ白だったもの。こん
な風にきれいに入ると嬉しくなる。

1. Mikiko's well-used small kohiki milk jug. Stains
and kan-nyuu have added character. 2. A matt
white cup with kan-nyuu. The cup was smooth and
pure white when bought. Fine kan-nyuu patterns
like these are a delight to the owner's eyes.

粉引・白マットの器の作り手を訪ねる 井山三希子さん

Visiting Mikiko Iyama / Maker of kohiki and matte white ware

「日々使う道具なのだから、白いものがいいと思う」

　井山三希子さんの作る姿勢は、明快で気持ちがいい。小さい頃から、何事にもこだわりが強かったと言う。絵付けなどに興味はなく、自分の好みでないものは持たないほうがいいと妥協しない。その井山さんの潔さは、作る器に表れている。色は白と黒が中心。かたちは円心系に回る効率のいいろくろではなく、型にこだわる。

　白にこだわりながらも、それは貫入との戦いでもあった。井山さん自身は、貫入は土の性質によるものだし、受け入れるべきものと思っている。しかし、使う人は千差万別。土を扱う人間ならわかりきっている貫入を、不良品のように思う人もいる。作り手が信頼するお店が説明しても、「永遠に白いまま」だと、思い違いをして買うお客もいる。粉引よりは貫入の入りにくい半磁器の白マットを、温度を上げて焼き、強度を持たせるなどと試行錯誤を続けているが、やはり入るものは入る。陶器とは、素材の中を顕微鏡で見たら、スカスカのスポンジのようなものなのだから。

　貫入に法則はない。貫入は器使いの醍醐味。ぜひそれを理解して楽しみたいものだ。

"I think white is the best color for daily tableware," says Mikiko Iyama.

　Her approach to her work is straightforward and refreshing. She says that she has had uncompromising tastes since a young age. She has no interest in decorating her ceramics and would rather not to have things that are not her taste or style. Mikiko's works reflect her clear-cut character. Black and white are the main colors she uses for her ceramics. Instead of using a turning wheel for more efficient work, she sticks to molds.

　Mikiko's persistence on making white pottery and her battle with kan-nyuu (fine crackles in ceramic vessels) go hand-in-hand. For Mikiko, kan-nyuu is part of the nature of clay and she thinks it should be accepted as it is. However everyone has their own opinion and some see kan-nyuu as a defect. Conscientious shop owners explain to their customers about kan-nyuu, but some still buy the ceramics believing "the white will stay as white forever." Mikiko has been experimenting with matte white semi-porcelain, which is less prone to kan-nyuu, firing at higher temperatures to improve its density. It has been trial and error but kan-nyuu still happens. Pottery is porous after all. Under a microscope, it looks like a sponge.

　There are no rules for kan-nyuu and that is what is thrilling about owing ceramic vessels. Kan-nyuu should be understood better and appreciated more.

1.底面に、スタンプで生地を作った日の日付を入れる。2.器のかたちは、この石膏型を使って作る。

1.After bisque firing, Mikiko stamps the date on the back of each piece. 2.Mikiko uses these plaster molds to create the shapes of her bowls.

1.粉引の飯碗（深）。最近は白マットの注文のほうが多いそうだが、ご飯茶碗は温かみがある粉引の
ほうが良い気がする。**2.**黒マットのオーバルプレート。ホウレンソウの緑、トマトソースの赤、卵料理
の黄色など、黒は色を引き立たせ、よりおいしそうに見せる。**3.**白マットの面取りボウルは常に人気
の品。**4.**耐熱の目玉焼きパン。井山さんのセンスが光る独特なかたち。

1.Deep kohiki rice bowl. Although matte white is becoming more popular, a warm touch of
kohiki seems more suitable for serving rice. **2.**Matte black oval plate. The green in spinach, red in
tomatoes, yellow in yolks; black highlights other colors and makes any dish look more appealing and
appetizing. **3.**This matte white faceted bowl is an ever-popular item. **4.**Heat-resistant ceramic frying
pan. The unique shape shows Mikiko's artistic sense of style.

作り手の使い方

井山さん定番のミートソースパスタと自家製
ピクルスは、粉引の器に盛りつける。もち
ろん両方とも水に浸してから盛りつけた。
こうすれば色の強いトマトソースもシミにな
らない。グラスはガラス作家の辻和美さん
のもの。

How the makers use it

Pasta with meat sauce, Mikiko's staple dish,
and homemade pickled vegetables are served
on kohiki plates. The plates were soaked in
water before placing the food. This prevents
the plate from being stained by the dark
tomato sauce. The cup was created by glass
artist Kazumi Tsuji.

安藤雅信の

銀彩の器

Silver Overglaze Ware / Masanobu Ando

銀彩ダイス深皿　Silver Overglaze Pewter Deep Dice Plate

素材 Materials	ストーンウェア、銀彩 Stoneware, Silver overglaze	
サイズ Dimensions	直径26.5×高さ4cm D26.5 x H4cm	
主な取扱い店 Stockist	ギャルリももぐさ Galerie Momogusa	

その他のラインナップ Product Information

銀彩シリーズには、ダイス皿、リム皿、輪花皿、スープ皿などがある。ほかに、オランダシリーズ、イタリアシリーズ、イギリスシリーズなどもある。

The silver overglaze series includes dice plates, rimmed plates, rinka (petal-shaped edge) plates and soup plates. Holland series, Italian series, England series are also available.

銀彩は、銀食器と同じような変化が
起こってくる。使わないで置いておく
だけだと、黄色から黒くなる。これは
サビではなく硫化だ。銀が空気中の硫
黄分と反応して起こる現象。安藤雅信
さんは硫化したものを「変化したのも
良い色でしょう」と見せてくれた。特に
使い込んでの色の変化は、使った人そ
れぞれの味わいが出てくる。

黒さが気になる場合、安藤さんは歯
磨き粉で磨く方法もすすめているが、
かなり地道な作業だ。一気に黒さを
取りたいときは、銀磨きを使うといい。
とはいえ、漆の修理と同じく、きれい
にすることで取れてしまった変化を同
じように再現するのは難しい。磨く前
によく考えたい。

Silver overglaze ware changes color
over time, similar to silverware. If it is
left unused, the silver color will change
to yellow and eventually turn black.
This is sulfide staining, not rusting, as
silver reacts with sulfur compounds in
the air. Masanobu Ando showed me
a tarnished piece and said, "Doesn't it
have a lovely color?" The color change,
especially in well-loved silverware, is
a part of the character it develops over
time and is as unique as its owner.

If the darkening is not wanted,
Masanobu recommends polishing
with toothpaste, although it is quite
time consuming. If you prefer a quick
solution, use a silver polish. But give
some thought before you do this
because once you have cleaned and
polished your silverglaze ware, the
patina will not come back so quickly.

特別な手入れ Occasional care

1 黒くなった状態が気になる場合は、重曹をつけて指でこすって磨き、水ですすぐ。

If you are bothered by blackening or discoloration, apply baking soda to the affected area and rub with fingers. Rinse the plate with water.

2 あるいは、ハギレに歯磨き粉をつけて磨き、水ですすぐ。重曹より時間はかからない。もちろん銀磨きを使っても。

An alternative is to put toothpaste on an old cloth and polish the affected area and rinse with water. This takes less time than using baking soda. A silver polish can also be used.

やってはいけないこと
DON'TS

| 電子レンジ Microwave | 食洗機 Dishwasher | 金属タワシ Metallic scrubber | 天日干し Dry in direct sunlight |

温泉卵をのせてはいけない。
Do not put onsen tamago (eggs poached in the shell) on the plate.

山本忠正の

土鍋

Donabe Clay Pot / Tadamasa Yamamoto

鉄釉土鍋尺	Tetsuyu (iron glaze) Donabe Shaku
素材 Material	耐火土 Fire clay
サイズ Dimensions	直径36×高さ17.5cm D36 × H17.5cm
主な取扱い店 Stockists	ギャラリーやまほん ギャラリーうつわノート Analogue Life Gallery Yamahon Gallery Utsuwa-note Analogue Life

その他のラインナップ Product Information

釉薬は飴釉や白もある。アイテムは土鍋ではごはん鍋、煮込み鍋など。そのほかに器も作っている。なかでも半磁器のレンゲは人気アイテム。

The glaze also comes in ameyu (amber brown) and white. Other donabe products available include rice cookers and casserole. Tadamasa also makes tableware and semi-porcelain "renge" spoons are one of the popular items among his works.

土を焼いてできる陶器。同じ土のはずなのに、直火にかけられるものとかけられないものがある。それは、熱膨張すると、ものは割れることに関係する。熱膨張係数が低くて、窯で焼いても焼き締まらない（＝割れにくい）土が、土鍋土として使われるのだ。

土鍋は購入したらまず、おもゆを作って「目止め」をする。このとき、底に必ずヒビが入る。このヒビは、落としてできたヒビとは違う。磁器や普通の陶器は、直火にかけると膨張に耐えきれずに割れるが、三重県伊賀の土で作った土鍋は違う。伊賀の土の特徴でもある微細な有機物（亜炭など）を含んだ粘土が、焼成することで微細な穴（多孔質）になり、割れを少しでくい止める。これがたくさんできることで、より耐熱性能が高まるという特徴がある。

使いはじめはおもゆを作ることで「慣らす」。最初のこの慣らしで、さっそく底にヒビが入るが、割れているのではないので安心を。このときに、決して強火で炊いてはいけない。強火だと外側だけが温まり、内側と温度差が生じて膨張率が変わってしまい、ヒビではなく、割れる可能性が出てくる。「良いヒビ」を作るのが土鍋と長く付き合う秘訣なのだ。

土の道具 …… 土鍋

Pottery is made by baking clay at a high temperature. Clay all seems the same but some pottery can be used over direct flame and others cannot. This is because stress within a ceramic body due to thermal expansion can cause fracture. The clay used for donabe has a low thermal expansion coefficient and does not harden too much when baked in a kiln (thus less prone to breakage).

When you have a new donabe, it needs "medome" or a sealing process by cooking omoyu (rice gruel or thick paste-like cooked rice) in it. During this process, the donabe gets cracks but these cracks are different from the ones when accidently dropped. Porcelain and common pottery cannot withstand the stress caused by high temperature thermal expansion and break. This is not the case with the donabe made from Iga clay from Mie prefecture. Iga clay contains microscopic organic matter (such as bytownite), which is unique to the clay in this region. When the clay is fired at a high temperature, this organic matter burns away to form tiny air pockets (become porous) that minimize cracks in donabe. The more air pockets the donabe has, the more heat resistant it becomes.

When the donabe is "seasoned" by cooking omoyu, it gets cracks. But rest assured, it does not mean the donabe is broken. Just make sure you do not cook omoyu over high heat. While low or medium heat allows the donabe to warm up from the center, high heat only warms the outside of the donabe creating a difference in temperature between the inside and the outside. This changes the thermal expansion coefficient of the donabe and increases the risk of fracturing. Making "good cracks" is the secret to enjoying your donabe for many years.

使いはじめ Before first use

1 おもゆ（米粒がなくドロドロした液体）を作る。小さめの鍋に水とご飯を入れて火にかける。

To make omoyu porridge (rice gruel), place cooked rice and water in a small saucepan and turn on the heat.

4 沸騰したら火を止め、冷めたら温めてを2〜3回繰り返す。

Bring it to a boil and then turn off the heat. Let it cool down and heat it up again. Repeat the process 2-3 times.

2 米粒が溶けてなくなったらおもゆのできあがり。

When the rice grains have turned into paste, the omoyu porridge is done.

5 おもゆを捨てて水洗いをし、布巾で拭く。

Discard the omoyu porridge and wash the donabe with water. Wipe dry with a cloth.

3 2を土鍋に移し、中弱火にかける。

Transfer the omoyu to the donabe pot. Place over heat to medium-low heat.

日々の手入れ Daily care

1 タワシかスポンジに中性洗剤をつ
けて洗う。

Wash the donabe with a mild detergent
and a tawashi or a sponge.

4 日当りのいい場所に置いて、しっか
りと乾かす。

Place the donabe in a sunny spot to dry
completely.

2 水かぬるま湯で洗剤をすすぐ。

Rinse with cold or lukewarm water.

5 カビ防止のため、底を上にして置
き、空気が流れる場所にしまう。

To prevent mold, store the donabe
upside down in a place with good
airflow.

3 布巾で拭いて水気を取る。

Wipe dry with a cloth.

困ったときは Troubleshooting

ヒビから漏れるとき
Leakage from the cracks

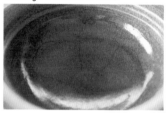

1 P72「使いはじめ」1〜2の方法で
おもゆを作り、土鍋に移す。

Make omoyu porridge following steps
1 and 2 on Page 72. Transfer the
porridge to the donabe.

2 最初は中弱火にかけ、温まったら強
火にし、沸騰したら火を止める。

Place the donabe over medium-low
heat and turn up to high once the
omoyu porridge is warmed up. Bring
to a boil and turn off the heat.

3 半日〜1日おいたらおもゆを捨てて
水で洗う。それでも漏れる場合は、
1〜3を何回か繰り返す。

Leave for a half day or whole day.
Discard the porridge and wash the
donabe with water. If the leaking
continues, repeat the process 1-3
several times.

焦げついたとき
Burnt on food

1 洗っても焦げが取れなかったら、
土鍋に水を張る。

If burnt on food does not come off by
washing, fill the donabe with water.

2 火にかけて沸騰したら火を止める。
そのまま1時間ほどおくと、焦げが
浮いてくる。

Place the donabe over heat. When it
boils, turn off the heat. Leave for about
one hour. The burnt on food should
come off and float to the surface.

やってはいけないこと
DON'TS

食洗機	金属タワシ	急冷
Dishwasher	Metallic scrubber	Rapid cooling

土鍋の底にできるヒビ
Cracks on the bottom of the donabe

写真上のヒビを見たら、誰でも「割れている」と思うだろう。しかし、これはごく普通のヒビの入り方だ。使い込んでいくうちに、ヒビの様子がわかってくる。漏れたと思っても、P72のようにおもゆを炊けば、止まることが多い。使いはじめは、とにかく強火禁止！ 強火で熱膨張に偏りが生じると、鍋も悲鳴を上げて割れる。ちなみに写真の土鍋はご飯鍋。

Anyone who sees the cracks shown in the photograph would think "the donabe is broken." But it is quite normal to have this kind of cracks on donabe. You will get to know the condition of your donabe as you use it. Even if your donabe starts to leak, you can often fix it by cooking omoyu porridge following the steps in Page 72. Make sure not to place it over high heat. The stress imbalance due to high temperature thermal expansion can badly fracture your donabe. The donabe shown in the photograph is for cooking rice.

土鍋の作り手を訪ねる

Visiting Tadamasa Yamamoto / Maker of donabe clay pots

　三重県伊賀の「やまほん陶房」の工房主を務める山本忠正さんは、個人で作家活動もしている。工房の土鍋は機械ろくろ（といっても、すべて人がついて作業し、熟練の技も要る、かなりアナログな道具）を使っているが、作家としては手ろくろで鍋を引いている。忠正さんは腕もいいが舌もいい。伊賀はおいしいものが多い土地ではあるが、山本家の食卓は格別だ。

　奥さんのこずえさんとは美大時代に出会った仲。美大といえども土とは無関係の暮らしだったこずえさんは、「土鍋素人」の代表選手。今では土鍋使いも慣れたものだが、最初は失敗の連続で、ヒビが入った、焦げた、と大騒ぎだったらしい。その驚きと発見をイラストにまとめ、忠正さんの鍋に添えて販売している。

　伺った日は、山本家で使い込まれた土鍋を使って鳥鍋をいただいた。少量の油で鶏肉を炒め、水も入れずに煮るので肉にうまみがぎゅっと凝縮している。土鍋ほど使いはじめと慣れてきたものと、使い勝手が違うものもないだろう。良いヒビ（P75参照）が入ることで、どんどん丈夫になる。そうすると、水を入れずに煮炊きしても、食材から出る水分程度でもうまく熱膨張し、割れることはないのだ。

Tadamasa Yamamoto runs Yamahon pottery workshop in Iga City, Mie Prefecture, and also works as a pottery artist. At the workshop, donabe pots are made by machine wheels (although each step in the process is supervised and needs an experienced hand) and Tadamasa uses a hand-turned wheel to make his personal works. Tadamasa has great skills in pottery and nice tastes in food. Iga is known for many delicacies and his household has exceptionally good food.

Tadamasa and his wife Kozue have been together since art college. Although she studied various art forms, Kozue knew nothing about clay back then. She started as a total "donabe beginner" with series of dramas of cracks and burnt on food. She is now a master of donabe. Kozue has illustrated her donabe cooking experiences with her own drawings and included in the instruction leaflet for Tadamasa's donabe.

When I visited Tadamasa and Kozue at home, I was treated to "torinabe" (chicken hot pot) cooked in one of Tadamasa's well-used donabe. They cooked meat with a small amount of oil first and cooked it further without adding water to the donabe. The meat was packed with flavor. There is such a big difference between a brand-new donabe and a well-used donabe when it comes to cooking. Donabe becomes stronger by getting "good" cracks with use (see Page 75) and tolerates thermal expansion allowing food to cook in its own juices.

1.ろくろでかたち作った後、必ず削る。2.伊賀土には雰囲気のある釉薬をかける。3.窯に入っているのは緑釉の土鍋。レールのついた荷台に土鍋をのせ、窯に入れる。

1.After being shaped on the pottery wheel, the pot is always trimmed. 2.Glaze is applied to the Iga clay to create nuances. 3.Green glazed donabes in the kiln. They are carried on a platform with rails into the kiln.

1.無水料理は鍋をある程度使い込んでからすること。使い慣れてくると「そろそろ無水でも大丈夫」とわかってくる。使い込まれた鍋は飴釉のもの。飴釉は光沢があり、食材がこびりつきにくい。油をちょっと入れた後に肉を入れ、そして野菜。肉のうまみがぎゅっと詰まった最高の味わいになる。2.ご飯ももちろん土鍋で炊く。蓋を重くして二重蓋と同等の圧力がかかるようにした。煮立って火を弱め、数分で火を止めて蒸らすと、最高においしいご飯が炊きあがる。

1.Cooking using a small amount of (or no) liquid should only be tried after the donabe has had considerable use. You will know when your donabe is ready. This is a well-used ameyu glazed donabe. Ameyu glaze creates a glossy look and helps prevent food from sticking. Add a small amount of oil in the donabe and cook the meat first and the vegetables. The meat is full of flavor and tastes superb. 2.As might be expected, rice is also cooked in donabe. This donabe has a heavy lid to create the same pressure as using a double lid. When it comes to a boil, reduce the heat to low and turn it off after a couple of minutes. Let stand for a while and the scrumptiously cooked rice is ready to serve.

作り手の使い方

こずえさんの得意料理は、忠正さんの土鍋で作る伊賀豚のローストポーク。あまりにおいしいのでレシピを教わった。作り方は、豚肩ロースに塩をすり込み、胡椒をまぶし、ローズマリーをつけてしばらくおく。フライパンにオリーブオイルを熱し、肉を一面ずつ焼きつける。すべての面が焼けたら、肉を土鍋に移して中央に置き、その周りにひと口大に切った季節の根菜を並べる。200度で予熱しておいたオーブンを250度にして土鍋ごと入れ、約20分焼く（800gの肉の場合）。火が入ったら、肉の繊維と垂直に切ってできあがり。

How the makers use it

Kozue's signature dish is roast Iga-pork cooked in Tadamasa's donabe. It was so delicious that I asked her for the recipe. Preheat the oven to 200 degrees. Rub salt into pork shoulder. Sprinkle pepper, put some rosemary on the meat and leave for a while. Heat olive oil in a frying pan and brown the meat on each of its sides. Transfer the meat to the middle of the donabe. Cut root vegetables in season into bite-size pieces and arrange around the meat. Increase the oven temperature to 250 degrees and put the donabe in the oven. Cook for about 20 minutes (for 800g meat). When the meat is done, slice against the grain and serve.

一陽窯の

備前焼の器

Bizen Ware / Ichiyougama

火襷7寸鉢 Hidasuki (straw fire marks) 21㎝ Bowl	
素材 Material	炻器 Sekki stoneware
サイズ Dimensions	直径21×高さ7cm D21 x H7cm
主な取扱い店 Stockists	一陽窯 ギャラリー栂 Ichiyougama Gallery Toga

その他のラインナップ Product Information

宝瓶、ビールコップ、コーヒーカップ&ソーサーなどの日用食器のほか、昔から硬くて評判のすり鉢もある。抹茶碗などの茶道具も揃う。

Daily-use kitchenware available includes houhin teapots, beer cups, coffee cups and saucers. Their grinding bowl (mortar) is well known for its hard surface. Japanese tea ceremony utensils including maccha tea bowls are also available.

備前焼とは炻器の一種。急須で有名な常滑焼や萬古焼も炻器だ。炻器の原料の粘土は、釉薬なしでも焼き締まり、水漏れしない特性がある。

　原料不足や生産効率を優先させるために、その土地の土を使う産地は減る一方だが、備前焼は土あってのもの。地元の田んぼの下の土を精製して寝かせ、それを薪窯で1週間以上も焼成したものは、「焼き締まった」独特の風合いを出す。扱いは比較的楽だが、急な温度変化は苦手。直火はもちろん、煮沸したり熱湯をかけると、割れる可能性がある。ただし、備前の焼き締まりは多孔質で、備長炭が水を浄化するのと同じような作用がある。兵糧攻めにあった兵士が、備前焼のかめの水が腐らなかったから長く戦えたほどだということだ。

日々の手入れ Daily care

使う前
Before use

油や食べ物の色がつくのを防ぐため、料理を盛る前に2〜5分ほど水に浸す。

Soak the bowl in water for 2-5 minutes before use to prevent oil and food stains.

Bizen ware is a type of sekki (Japanese stoneware). There are other sekki ware in Japan such as Tokoname ware, well known for its tea pots, and Banko ware. The characteristics of the clay used for sekki pottery are that it hardens without glazing and holds liquid.

Due to a shortage of raw materials and an emphasis on efficient production, the number of pottery producers using their local clay has been decreasing. For Bizen pottery, the clay plays the most crucial part. After being dug from under local rice fields, the clay is refined and rests. It is then fired for over a week in a wood-fire kiln creating the distinctive "yakishime" (baked and hardened) texture and look. Although Bizen ware does not require special handling, it does not take a sudden change in temperature

very well. Putting in boiling water or pouring hot water over it, let alone placing over direct heat, can cause breakage. Bizen yakishime ware (high-fired unglazed stoneware) is porous and is said to be able to purify water in the same way "binchotan" charcoal (traditional Japanese charcoal) does. An old story tells that besieged soldiers were cut off from their food supply but were able to continue fighting thanks to the Bizen pot that kept their water fresh.

やってはいけないこと
DON'TS

| 電子レンジ Microwave | 食洗機 Dishwasher | 金属タワシ Metallic scrubber | 熱湯 Boiling water |

金属の道具
Metal Utensils

金属の加工は鍛金、鋳金、彫金の3つに分けられる。

鍛金は「叩く」仕事。

叩きながら金属を変形させるが、金属を伸ばすプレス加工と、

徐々に金属を寄せながら変形させる絞りの作業がある。

鋳金は「鋳物」。金属をドロドロに溶かし、

型に流し入れることでかたち作る。

彫金はアクセサリーや装飾品を作ることが多いが、

鏨やルーターなどの道具を使って、

図柄を彫ったり、透かし彫りをしたりする技術。

これらの技法を少しでも頭に入れておくと、

身近に使っていた生活道具に、また違う興味がわいてくる。

Metal working is divided into three categories: forging, casting and metal engraving. Forging is the hammering. It involves press work to stretch the metal and raising to form the metal shape by gradually pulling it together. Casting or "metal casting" involves melting metal into liquid and pouring it into a mold to form a shape. Metal engraving is often used to make accessories and ornaments but this method is also used with a tool such as a graver or a router to carve designs or to create openwork. Knowing a little about these methods can spark a new interest in the tools we use every day.

成田理俊の
鍛鉄のフライパン

Wrought Iron Frying Pan / Takayoshi Narita

フライパン、フライ返し Frying Pan, Frying Turner

素材 Material	鉄 Iron
サイズ Dimensions	フライパン:直径20.6×持ち手含む長さ35.2×高さ8.3㎝ フライ返し:長さ(柄含む) 33㎝ Frying Pan: D20.6 x L(including the handle)35.2 x H8.3㎝ Turner: L(including the handle)33㎝
主な取扱い店 Stockists	夏椿 in-kyo くるみの木cage Natsutsubaki in-kyo Kuruminoki cage

その他のラインナップ
Product Information

フライパンは他に27㎝、24
㎝、22㎝、18㎝、17㎝、15
㎝の計7サイズある。両手
パン、アジアンパンもある。

The frying pan is available
in 7 seizes in total: 27㎝,
24㎝, 22㎝, 18㎝, 17㎝
and 15㎝. Two handle
pans and Asian pans are
also available.

84

　成田理俊さんは、鉄板を一枚ずつ燃え盛るコークス（石炭を原料とした燃料）炉の中に入れ、出してはハンマーで叩き、また炉の中に入れ……を何十回も繰り返し、フライパンを作る。このように打ちつけて鉄を成形する技法が「鍛鉄」だ。ただ、このような手作りのフライパンは少ない。それは、作る工程が大変だから。成田さんは最適だと思う1.6㎜と2.3㎜の厚さに、鉄板を何度も叩いて作る。鉄でも軽くて扱いやすいのが人気の秘訣だ。

　鉄はそのままだとすぐに赤サビが出るが、成田さんはサビ防止のために、蜜蝋とエゴマ油をブレンドして作った自然素材の特製ワックスを塗っているのも特徴だ。そのまま食べても大丈夫な素材のため、一般の鉄のフライパンのように、使いはじめに焼き切る必要はない。

　成田さんのフライパンは、薄く作られている。強火に慣れている人がいつもの火加減で使うと、焦げつくので注意。火は中火か弱火で。鉄板が薄いうえ、鉄は元来熱伝導がいいので、充分に火は通る。鉄の組織に悪いため、急冷はしないこと。また、トマトにも注意が必要。これはトマトに代表される、酸味の強いものという意味。調理して、そのまま放置することは厳禁。せっかくついた黒皮（酸化皮膜）が取れてしまう可能性があるからだ。もちろんトマトを使って調理をしていいが、完成したら放置せず、早めに洗うことを心掛けよう。

Takayoshi Narita places an iron plate in the burning coke furnace. He takes it out and beats it with a hammer and puts it back in the furnace. He makes his wrought iron pans by repeating this forging process over and over. Handmade frying pans are rare these days because of this very time-consuming method. Takayoshi keeps beating the iron until it reaches to the thicknesses he thinks ideal for the pan: 1.6mm and 2.3mm. Easy-to-handle lightness is the secret of his highly popular iron pans.

　If iron is untreated, it rusts quite quickly. Takayoshi uses a special mixture of beeswax and egoma oil to coat his pans to prevent rust. It is all natural and safe to eat, and his iron pans do not require a burning-off process before using for the first time.

　Takayoshi's frying pans are quite thin. If you are used to cooking with high heat, be careful not to burn your foods. Use only medium or low heat. As the pan is thin and iron is a good conductor, enough heat goes through the food. Rapid cooling should be avoided because it damages the structure of iron. Cooking highly acidic food like tomatoes needs caution as well. The pan should not be left unwashed after the cooking is done because acidity in food left in the pan can peel off the protective black coating (oxide film). You can use your iron frying pan to cook any kind of food with tomatoes, just remember to wash it as soon as possible when you have finished.

使いはじめ Before first use

1 スポンジに中性洗剤をつけて洗う。水かぬるま湯ですすぎ、布巾で水気を拭き取る。

Wash the frying pan with a mild detergent and a sponge. Rinse with water or lukewarm water and wipe dry with a cloth.

2 弱火～中火にかけ、オリーブオイル大さじ1くらいを入れる。

Place the frying pan over low to medium heat and add about one tablespoon of olive oil.

3 野菜くずを入れて2～3分炒め、油をなじませたら、取り出す。
※野菜くずを炒めなくても使用可能だが、炒めたほうが油がなじんでいい。

Add vegetable scraps and stir-fry for 2-3 minutes. When the frying pan is seasoned, remove the vegetable scraps from the frying pan.
＊Stir frying vegetable scraps is not essential but improves the seasoning process.

日々の手入れ Daily care

1 使用後は手でさわれるくらいまでに冷めたら、スポンジに中性洗剤をつけて洗う。

When the frying pan is cool enough to touch after use, wash with a mild detergent and a sponge.

2 水かぬるま湯ですすぎ、弱火～中火にかけてしっかり水気を飛ばす。

Rinse with water or lukewarm water. Place the frying pan over low to medium heat to remove the remaining water.

86

特別な手入れ Occasional care

艶を出す
Giving the frying pan a glossy look

白っぽくなってきたら、キッチンペーパーなどにオリーブオイルを染み込ませて塗る。フライパンの裏面はガスの火が直接当たり、油も飛んでサビやすいので、裏面も塗る。ただし、頻繁に塗ると油が酸化し、焼くたびに油が層になって焦げつきやすくなるため、たまに塗る程度に。

When the color of the frying pan starts to turn cloudy and whitish, wipe with a paper towel dipped in olive oil. Also apply the oil to the back of the frying pan because it has direct contact with flame and tends to get rusty because of oil spills. This treatment should only be done occasionally. If it is done too often, it will cause oil oxidation and the frying pan will develop a layer of carbon and get burnt easily.

やってはいけないこと
DON'TS

電子レンジ Microwave	食洗機 Dishwasher	急冷 Rapid cooling

困ったときは Troubleshooting

焦げついたとき
Burnt on food

1 フライパンに水を張って弱火〜中火にかける。沸騰したら火を止め、30分ほどおく。

Fill the frying pan with water and place over low to medium heat. Bring to a boil and turn off the heat. Leave for about 30 minutes.

2 1の水を捨て、タワシでこすって焦げを落とす。取れにくい場合は、金属タワシを使ってもOK。

Discard the water and scrub the burnt area with a tawashi or a scrubbing brush. A metallic scourer can be used for stubborn stains.

サビたとき
Rust

スチールウールのタワシなどのサビ落としでこすって磨く。

Scrub off the rust with a steel wool scourer.

鍛鉄のフライパンの作り手を訪ねる　成田理俊さん

Visiting Takayoshi Narita / Maker of wrought iron frying pans

　誰かのひとことが大きな転機となることはしばしばある。成田理俊さんは、美大で絵画を学んだが、絵は辞め、立体に進む。造形会社に勤めた後、職業訓練校に入り、終了後は鉄工所に就職。独立して工房を作ったのは、風景が気に入った群馬県みなかみ町だった。最初は嗜好品ともいえるようなインテリアアイテムを作っていたが、あるクラフトフェアに参加したとき、主宰の女性にフライパンを作ってみたらとすすめられた。その意見を聞き入れない道もあったのだろうが、成田さんは挑戦してみた。できあがったのは、ほかにはない美しいかたちのフライパンだった。

　フライパンひとつに、いくつもの工夫を施している。表情をつけるために何度も火入れして、焼き肌をつけていたが、これがサビ止めの酸化皮膜になり、サビにくいフライパンができた。毎日使うものだから丈夫にしたいと、柄はほかの部分の鉄より炭素量の多い建築資材の丸棒をわざわざ叩いて伸ばしている。吊るして収納するための柄の穴は、3回叩き、めくれあがって見える。言われなければ気づかないほどの微妙なめくれ具合だが、こういうディテールにもこだわっているのが成田さんのフライパンなのだ。

A turning point in a person's career can often be triggered by a comment from somebody. Takayoshi Narita was an art student who studied painting and then switched to formative art. He worked for an art and design company before going to vocational school and finding employment at an iron foundry. Later, Takayoshi decided to work independently and opened his own studio. He chose Minakami town in Gunma prefecture because he loved the scenery. Takayoshi was making luxury furniture until one day he took part in a craft fair. At the fair an organizer suggested he make iron frying pans. He could have just ignored her advice, but decided to take the challenge. The result was a frying pan with a distinctively beautiful shape.

A number of Takayoshi's innovative ideas are incorporated into his frying pan. For example, he bakes the pan in fire many times to give the iron a more defined look, and this process also allows an oxide film to form on the surface making the pan more rust resistant. Because frying pans are used daily, Takayoshi wants them to be durable. He uses a building material iron rod with higher carbon content to make the handle and takes the trouble hammering by hand to stretch it. A hanging hole for storage is made by hammering three times and is slightly turned upward. It is so subtle that few would notice, but this attention to detail is what makes Takayoshi's pan so special.

丸棒から板状にすると
いう途方もない作業を
して、柄を作る。

The handle is made by
flattening an iron rod
with a hammer. It is a
painstaking process.

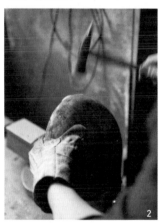

1.熱い鉄を叩いているのは、鉄に表情をつける作業だが、酸化皮膜がつき、サビ止めにもなる。2.叩いて側面を作っていく作業。3.フライパンの持ち手の変化。右側の丸棒が原型で、左へいくにしたがって柄に近づいていく。平らにしたのち、一番左の中が空洞の持ち手になる。

1.Takayoshi hammers a heated iron pan to give a more defined look to the surface. This process also gives an oxide film which provides protection against rust. 2.Hammering work to shape the sides. 3.The transformation from a rod to a handle. On the far right is the raw material, a cylindrical rod. To the left shows how the work progresses. After the rod is flattened, it is formed into a hollow handle, shown on the far left.

作り手の使い方

工房で自分のフライパンを
使って料理することもたび
たび。**1.**黒いフライパンに
黄色がまぶしいオムレツ
は、かたちができたら弱火
にして仕上げる。器には移
さず、このまま食卓に出し
て食べたくなる美しさだ。
2.おいしい焦げ目がつく餃
子は、火から外すタイミン
グがポイント。蓋は陶器の
作家のものを使っている。

How the makers use it

Takayoshi often cooks in his
workshop using his frying
pan. **1.**The black frying pan
complements the yellow
golden omelet. To make an
omelet like this, finish on
low heat when the eggs take
shape. It looks so delicious
and is beautiful enough to
serve straight to the table.
2.Removing the frying pan
from the heat at the right
time is the key to making
golden brown gyoza (pan-
fried dumplings). Takayoshi
uses a lid made by a ceramic
artist.

1
2

及源鋳造の

南部鉄器

Nambu Ironware / Oigen Foundry

鉄瓶 丸釜大アラレ（小）
クックトップ 丸深形 中20㎝

Nambu Tetsubin Iron Kettle Round Oarare (small)
Cooktop Deep Round Casserole medium 20㎝

素材 Material	鋳鉄 Cast iron
サイズ Dimensions	鉄瓶：縦16.7×横19.5×高さ19.2㎝ クックトップ：縦17.9×横24.7×高さ13㎝ Tetsubin Iron Kettle: L16.7 x W19.5 x H19.2cm Cooktop Casserole: L17.9 x W24.7 x H13cm
主な 取扱い店 Stockists	日本橋 木屋本店（鉄瓶） 私の部屋（クックトップ） Nihonbashi Kiya Main Store (Tetsubin iron kettle) Watashi no Heya (Cooktop casserole)

その他のラインナップ Product Information

鉄瓶はデザイン違いが多数あり。クックトップは直径24㎝、
15㎝もある。ほかに、丸鍋、すき焼鍋、タミさんのパン焼器、
グリル鉄板など多数のアイテムがある。

The tetsubin kettle comes in various designs. The cooktop
casserole also comes in 24cm and 15cm in diameter.
Many other products are available including round pots,
sukiyaki nabe pots, Tami pan (cast iron ring pan) and
iron griddles.

経済産業省の伝統的工芸品に指定されている南部鉄器は、高温で溶かした鉄を型に流し込んでかたち作る「鋳鉄」だ。及源の製造現場を見せてもらうと、工場とはいえひとつひとつが手作業なのに驚く。砂でできた型に溶かした鉄を流し込み、バリ（余分な鉄が型からあふれてできた羽根のようなもの）を取り、サビ止めをしてできあがる。熱く、堅い素材の加工は危険と隣り合わせだが、ほかにはない堅牢さと重厚感を併せ持つ。南部鉄器は海外でも人気だ。伝統工芸士が作る鉄瓶は、窯で焼いて酸化皮膜をつけ、漆などで黒く着色する。鍋などの油を使う道具は、一般的にはカシューなどの塗料を焼きつける。

同じ鉄で作っていても、この２つは使い方がまったく違う。鉄鍋は油を使うが、鉄瓶は水を沸かす道具のため油を使うことはない。これにより、手入れの方法も大きく異なるのだ。

鉄鍋は使い込んでいくうちに油が染み込んでいくため、油がサビ止めの作用をすることになる。一方、鉄瓶の手入れは触らぬことだ。鉄瓶の内部にサビ止めの酸化皮膜をつけるために、窯で焼く作業を施す（P100写真1）。この酸化皮膜や、水を沸かすと自然につく湯垢という天然のサビ止めが剥がれるのを防ぐためだ。そもそも水しか沸かさないのだから、洗う必要はない。余熱で蒸気を飛ばせば、お手入れ完了だ。

Nambu tekki cast iron is one of the officially certified traditional crafts of Japan. It is made by pouring molten iron into molds. On a visit to the Oigen foundry, I was surprised to see that each stage of the manufacturing process involved some hands-on work. The workers pour molten iron into sand molds, remove burrs (raised rough edges made by excess iron) and apply a rust-proof coating to finish. Handling hot and hard metal is clearly dangerous work but the casting process gives a strong presence to Nambu tekki ironware that has gained worldwide popularity. The traditional Nambu tekki craftsmen make iron kettles by firing in a furnace to oxide the matal and applying black urushi lacquer to finish. For other iron cookware including cast iron cooking pots that are used with oil, cashew nuts shell coating is burned into the surface.

Although they are made of the same material, the iron pot and the iron kettle require different handling and care. While the iron kettle is used only for boiling water, the iron pot is often used with oil.

The inside of the pot will be gradually sealed with the oil and this prevents rust. The iron kettle on the other hand has been baked in a kiln (photograph 1 in Page 100) to give the inside an oxide film to prevent rust and lime scale built-up inside of the kettle also provides rust protection. These coatings should not be removed. The kettle is used only for boiling water therefore cleaning is not necessary. Just remove the moisture inside the kettle using the remaining heat, and the maintenance is complete.

鉄瓶の場合　Iron kettle

使いはじめ Before first use

1 水かぬるま湯で中を軽くすすぐ。

Rinse the inside of the kettle with water or lukewarm water.

2 中に水を入れて中火にかけて、沸騰させる。

Fill the kettle with water. Place over medium heat and bring to a boil.

3 沸騰した湯を捨て、再び水を入れて沸かす。これを3回繰り返して、湯に「慣らす」。

Discard the water. Repeat step 2 three times to "season" the kettle.

日々の手入れ Daily care

1 使用後は、蓋をとって中火にかけ、30秒ほど空焚きして水気を飛ばす。

After use, place the empty kettle over medium heat without the lid. Leave for 30 seconds to remove the remaining water.

2 蓋は逆さまにしておくと乾きが早くなる。

Turn the lid upside down to dry faster.

注意すること Caution

湯を沸かしているときは蓋をずらすか外す。沸騰時の吹きこぼれを防ぐため。

Leave the lid ajar or off while boiling to prevent the water from boiling over.

特別な手入れ Occasional care

風合いを出す
Adding texture

1 お茶でパッティングすると独特な風合いが出る。まずは緑茶を布巾に浸す。

Patting with green tea adds character to the kettle. First, add tea to a dry cloth.

2 鉄瓶が温かいうちに、鉄瓶の表面を1の布巾でパンパンと叩くようにしてパッティングする。

While the kettle is still warm, pat the exterior with the tea-soaked cloth.

やってはいけないこと
DON'TS

 電子レンジ Microwave 食洗機 Dishwasher 金属タワシ Metallic scrubber 天日干し Dry in direct sunlight

急冷 Rapid cooling

困ったときは Troubleshooting

赤い湯になったとき
Red rust

1 タワシで内部のサビた部分をこすり、すすぐ。

Scrub the rusted area with a tawashi or a scrubbing brush and rinse with water.

2 出がらしの緑茶をだしパックに詰めて鉄瓶に入れ、20分ほど湯を沸かし、火を止める。ひと晩おいて水を捨てる。

Fill an empty tea bag with used loose tea leaves and put it in the kettle with water. Let it boil for about 20 minutes and turn off the heat. Leave overnight and discard the contents.

3 湯の色が透明になったらOK。色がついていたら2を3回ほど繰り返してみる。

Boil water in the kettle to see if the water is clear. If not, repeat the step 2 about three times.

鉄鍋の場合　Iron pot

使いはじめ Before first use

1 水かぬるま湯で中を軽くすすぐ。

Rinse the inside of the pot with water or lukewarm water.

4 大さじ1ほどのオリーブオイルなどを入れて、火をつける。

Add one tablespoon of olive oil to the pot and turn the heat back on.

2 布巾でさっと水気を拭く。

Give a quick wipe dry with a cloth.

5 野菜くずを入れてしんなりするまで炒め、油をまんべんなくなじませる。

Cook vegetable scraps until they soften, blending the oil evenly in the pot.

3 強火にかけて水気を飛ばす。空焚きし続けるのは危険なので、乾いたら一旦、火を止める。

Place the pot over high heat to remove the remaining water. As soon as the pot is dry turn off the heat (leaving an empty pot on heat is dangerous).

6 手でさわれるくらいに冷めてから、野菜くずを捨ててタワシで洗う。火にかけて水気を飛ばす。

When the pot is cool enough to touch, discard the vegetable scraps and wash the pot with a tawashi or a scrubbing brush. Place the pot over heat to remove the remaining water.

日々の手入れ Daily care

1 使用後は手でさわれるくらいまで冷めてから、洗剤は使わずタワシで洗って、水ですすぐ。

When the pot has cooled down after use, wash with a tawashi or a scrubbing brush without using detergent. Rinse with water.

2 布巾で水気を拭き、強火にかけ、30秒ほど空焚きして水気を飛ばす。

Wipe the pot with a cloth and place over high heat. Leave for about 30 seconds to remove the remaining water.

困ったときは Troubleshooting

赤い点々 (サビ) が出たとき
Red spots (rust)

1 洗剤をつけずにタワシでゴシゴシこすって水ですすぐ。布巾で水気を拭き、強火にかけ30秒ほど空焚きして水気を飛ばす。

Scrub the red spots with a tawashi or a scrubbing brush without using detergent, and rinse with water. Wipe with a cloth and place over high heat. Leave for about 30 seconds to remove the remaining water.

2 大さじ1ほどのオリーブオイルなどを入れて火にかけ、野菜くずを炒める。点々が消えるまで1〜2を繰り返す。

Add about one tablespoon of olive oil to the pot, turn the heat on and cook vegetable scraps. Repeat the process 1-2 until the spots disappear.

やってはいけないこと
DON'TS

| 電子レンジ Microwave | 食洗機 Dishwasher | 金属タワシ Metallic scrubber | 天日干し Dry in direct sunlight |

| 急冷 Rapid cooling |

金属の道具

‥‥‥‥

南部鉄器

南部鉄器の作り手を訪ねる

及源鋳造

Visiting Oigen Foundry / Maker of nambu ironware

　南部鉄器は旧南部藩の盛岡と旧伊達藩の水沢で作られる鋳物だが、歴史は水沢のほうが古く、1090年頃といわれている。水沢にある及源鋳造の工場には製造の機械が点在するが、型に砂を詰める、鉄を流すなど、細部は人の手によるところが多い。職人は鉄が入った柄杓を持って、まるで水のように軽々と型に注ぎ込むが、発光する鉄の比重は水の7.3倍ととんでもなく重い。この重さだからできる鍋、この素材だからできる鉄瓶は、海外でも人気。マイナスと思われがちな重さが、堅牢な存在感として人を引きつけるのだ。「工場＝大量生産」と、考える人もいるが、及源の工場を見ると、多くの人ができるだけ手に入れやすい価格で、良質なものを作る努力が伝わってくる。さらに、環境にも配慮したいと、数年前から取り組んでいるのが、古来からの鉄瓶のサビ止め方法を鉄鍋に応用した、塗装をしない「上等鍋」だ。銀色の鉄を焼くと酸化皮膜がつく。それはブルーグレーをしていて、私たちの知っている黒い鉄とはほど遠いが、これが天然の塗装になるそうだ。及源鋳造の特許商品で、海外では無塗装鍋「Naked Pan」として販売されている。

Nambu tekki is cast ironware produced in Morioka of the former Nambu-han and in Mizusawa of the former Date-han. The history of the iron casing industry in Mizusawa goes back to around 1090, much earlier than that in Morioka. At the Oigen foundry in the city of Mizusawa, manufacturing machines are spotted inside but some detailed work such as filling molds with sand and pouring molten iron into the molds is carried out by hand. One of the workers carries a dipper filled with molten iron and pours it into the molds as if he were pouring water. The glowing iron liquid is extremely heavy, weighing 7.3 times more than water. The iron pots and kettles are popular overseas, particularly for their weight and material. The heaviness that some see as negative creates a strong presence that is attractive to many people.

　Some might simply assume that "factory equals mass production" but the effort to make high quality products with affordable price is evident at the Origen foundry. Furthermore, taking the impact on environment into consideration, they have been engaged in developing the non-coating iron pan, "Joto nabe" (high quality pans) for several years. They have applied an old rust prevention method used for the iron kettle from ancient times to produce this eco-friendly iron cookware. When silver iron is burnt it allows an oxide film to form on the surface. It is a blue gray color, nothing like common black iron oxide, and acts as a natural protective coating. The pans are patented and sold abroad as no additional coating "Naked Pan".

型から出したばかりの鉄瓶は銀色に輝いている。このままだとすぐに赤サビが出る。

When the iron kettles are just taken out of the molds, they have silvery shine. If left untreated, they will soon rust.

1.銀色の鉄は、酸化皮膜をつけるために灼熱の窯で焼かれる。2.作業の基本は手作業だ。3.伝統的な手作りの鉄瓶の型（焼き型）。

1.The silver iron kettles are fired in a scorching kiln to form an oxide film on the surface. 2.Hands-on work is the foundation of ironware making at the Oigen foundry. 3.Traditional hand-made molds for iron kettles (casting mold).

作り手の使い方

1.及源のショールームで、常にお湯を沸かしている鉄瓶。内側にぶ厚くついた湯垢に驚く人も少なくない。
2.オーブンがなくてもガスコンロで手軽に"パンケーキ"が焼ける「タミさんのパン焼器」。ショールームで焼いて、お客さんにふるまうことも。

How the makers use it

1.There is always water boiling in this iron kettle in the Oigen showroom. Visitors are often amazed with the thick lime scale build-up inside the kettle.
2.Even if you do not have an oven, you can easily bake a tea cake with "Tami Pan" (cast iron ring pan) on a gas stove top. The cakes are sometimes made at the showroom and offered to the visitors.

1
2

101

山田工業所の

中華鍋

Wok / Yamada Kogyosho

鉄片手鍋 Single Handle Iron Wok

素材 Material	鉄 Iron
サイズ Dimensions	直径27×高さ8cm、鉄の厚さ1.2mm D27 x H8cm, Thickness 1.2mm
主な取扱い店	ナカタ 和田食器 青木商事 千田
Stockists	Nakata Wada Shokki Aoki Shoji Senda

その他のラインナップ
Product Information

鉄片手鍋は8サイズ、鉄の厚さはほかに1.6mm、直径が63cm以上は2.3mmになる。ほかに、鉄両手鍋、鉄フライパン、鉄揚げ鍋、鉄餃子鍋など多数のアイテムがある。

The single handle iron wok comes in 8 sizes. It is also available with a thickness of 1.6mm, and 2.3mm for 63cm in diameter or larger. A wide range of products is available including two handle iron pans, iron frying pans, iron pots for deep-frying, iron pans for making gyoza(pan-fried dumplings).

山田工業所の創業は1957年。戦後、もののない時代でもドラム缶はあったので、それを叩いて中華鍋を作りはじめた。何度も叩くために凹凸ができ、油のなじみが良くなるこの鍋は、すぐに全国の料理人の間で評判になった。その後、1枚ずつ叩いていたら埒があかないと、すでに酸化皮膜のついた鉄板を10枚重ねて叩くプレスの機械を作り、時間は一気に短縮。そのうえ、10枚まとめて叩くことで組織が締まって強くなるため、プロの料理人の使用頻度にも耐えうる中華鍋ができるようになったのだ。

初めて中華鍋を見る人は、その艶に驚くだろう。これはニス（ワニスともいう）が塗ってあるから。ニスはサビ止めにほかならない。メーカーは大量に作って、信頼できる仲買人に卸すが、使い手に渡るまで見届ける訳にはいかない。ならば、しっかりと客に届くまでは、サビないようにニスでガードをしようということだ。だから、使いはじめるときは、ニスを「焼き切る」必要がある。ニスは熱で揮発していく。だが、ちょっと水分や塩分が残ると赤サビは出る。そのときは、サンドペーパーかスチールウールのタワシでサビを落とし、もう一度「慣らし」（P104参照）をすればいい。

社長の山田豊明さんは、「鉄は熱の通りが早いので、野菜はシャキッと炒められるよ」と中華鍋の利点を話す。「鉄分は摂れますか？」と質問すると「鉄のお玉とセットで使うと、鉄が削れてもっと摂れる」と答えてくれた。

Yamada Kogyosho was founded in 1957. In this post-war time there was shortage of everything, but plenty of drums, and that was what they used to start making their iron woks. Their method of hammering an iron plate over and over gave the wok an irregular surface and that helped cooking oil blend in with the iron. Their wok soon became popular among chefs all over Japan. As demand grew, they built a machine that could hammer ten oxide iron plates at a time. Manufacturing time was significantly reduced and, what's more, hammering thicker layers made the iron structure even stronger and they were able to produce a wok that could withstand heavy use by professionals.

If you have never seen a brand new wok before, you would be surprised by its waxy shine. It comes from the varnish, rust prevention. Manufacturers make numerous woks and sell them to wholesalers, but they never see the end users. So they varnish their woks to make sure they will stay rust-free for their customers. The varnish needs to be "burnt off" before the first use. It vaporizes by heating but if any moisture or salty residue is left, the wok will rust. If that happens, you can use sandpaper or a steel wool pad to remove the rust and "season" your wok again (see Page 104).

Toyoaki Yamada, managing director of Yamada Kogyosho, explains the benefits of cooking with a wok. "Iron conducts heat quickly, so you can make crunchy stir-fry vegetables." "Can I take iron from wok?" I asked. "Use an iron ladle with a wok. Iron particles will be scraped off from the surface and you will get more iron," said Mr. Yamada.

使いはじめ Before first use

1 中華鍋を強火にかけ、空焚きする。
熱がまんべんなく伝わるように手
首を回して動かしながら行う。

Place the empty wok over high heat.
Tilt the wok constantly to let the heat
spread evenly.

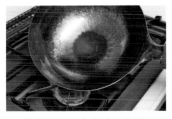

2 焼きはじめると表面が黒くなって
くる。

When the wok starts to burn, its
surface turns black.

4 鍋の温度が少し下がったら、タワシ
で洗って水ですすぐ。中性洗剤を
使ってもOK。

When the wok has cooled down
a little, wash with a tawashi or a
scrubbing brush and rinse with water.
A mild detergent can be used.

5 油（何でもOK）を大さじ2ほど入れ
て野菜くずを炒める。

Stir-fry vegetable scraps with two
tablespoons of cooking oil (any kind).

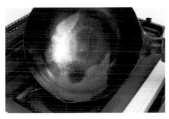

3 全体が灰色になったらニスを「焼き
切った」状態に。直径27㎝の中華
鍋で、ここまで1時間ほどかかる。

When the wok turns a silver grey all
over, it is the sign that the rust-proof
varnish has been burnt off. It takes
about one hour for a 27cm-diameter
wok to reach this condition.

6 鍋の温度が少し下がったら、野菜く
ずを捨て、タワシで洗ってすすぎ、
火にかけて水気を飛ばす。

When the wok has cooled down a
little, discard the vegetable scraps.
Wash the wok with a tawashi or a
scrubbing brush and rinse. Place over
heat to remove the remaining water.

日々の手入れ Daily care

1 使用後は、鍋の温度が少し下がったら、タワシで洗って水ですすぐ。中性洗剤を使ってもOK。

When the wok has cooled down a little after use, wash with a tawashi or a scrubbing brush and rinse with water. A mild detergent can be used.

2 強火にかけ、20秒ほど空焚きして水気を飛ばす。

Place the wok over high heat. Leave for about 20 seconds to remove the remaining water.

困ったときは Troubleshooting

赤サビが出たとき
Red rust

スチールウールのタワシや目の細かいサンドペーパーなどのサビ落としでこすって磨く。

Scrub off the rust with a steel wool scourer or sand with fine sandpaper.

金属の道具

⋯⋯⋯

中華鍋

やってはいけないこと
DON'TS

| 電子レンジ Microwave | 食洗機 Dishwasher |

アルミの鍋（無水鍋®）

Aluminum Pot (Musuinabe) / Seikatsu Shunju

無水鍋 20cm　Musuinabe 20cm

素材 Material	アルミニウム Aluminum
サイズ Dimensions	本体:内径20×深さ7.8cm　蓋:内径20×深さ3.4cm Pot: Inner D20 x Depth 7.8cm　Lid: Inner D20 x Depth 3.4cm
主な取扱い店	D&DEPARTMENT 212 KITCHEN STORE クロワッサンの店 東急ハンズ 松屋銀座デザインコレクション
Stockists	D&DEPARTMENT 212 KITCHEN STORE Kurowassan no Mise Tokyu Hands Matsuya Ginza Design Collection

その他のラインナップ Product Information

内径24cmのサイズのほか、IH対応加工のもの、ごはん鍋もある。

The musuinabe comes in 24cm inner diameter. Other products available include induction-safe pots and rice cookers.

鉄の鍋に鋳鉄と鍛鉄があるように、アルミにも両方の作り方がある。こちらの無水鍋は、鋳込みで作るアルミの塊の鍋だ。塊だから強い。だが、塊といっても軽い。無水鍋はぴったりと蓋が閉まり、蒸気を逃さない。そのため高温が一定に保たれ、加熱時間が短く済み、栄養を逃さない。食品に含まれる水分だけで調理ができるので、水を加えて味を薄めてしまうことがない。また、蓋はフライパン代わりに使える。

利点揃いではあるが、水の中の成分と反応して変化を起こすため、手入れにはほかの素材よりちょっとしたコツが必要だ。アルミはアルカリ性に反応するので、こんにゃくや生の中華麺（かんすい）を入れると、一度に真っ黒になることもあり、さらに、白いポツポツ＝白サビがついてくることもある。白サビはそんなに気にしなくてもいいが、進行しないようにはしたい。そのためには、白サビを誘発する水の汲み置きや水分が残ったまの放置は厳禁。「無水」鍋と名前を唱え、水を拭く癖をつけよう。

また、重曹は何でもきれいにすると思い込みがちだが、アルミは別。重曹で洗ってできた黒変化は手強い。重曹にも「アルミ製品には使わないように」と書かれている。無水鍋で米のとぎ汁を最初に煮るという手入れ（P108参照）は、アルミに皮膜を作り、「黒変化」の予防策となるのだ。

Like iron pots, there are two types of aluminum pots: cast and wrought. The musuinabe in the photograph is a cast aluminum pot. It is strong yet light. With a tightly fitting lid, the musuinabe does not allow steam to escape. It retains the heat at a high temperature, reduces cooking time and traps the nutrients of foods. The musuinabe allows the food cook with its own juices so the flavor will not be lost by adding water. The lid can also be used as a flying pan.

While it has many advantages, the musuinabe needs a little more care than utensils made of other materials because aluminum reacts with minerals in water. For example, it reacts with alkaline and the musuinabe may turn black instantly when food such as konnyaku (aum root) and fresh Chinese noodles (contains lye water) is cooked in it. The musuinabe may also have problems with white spots or white rust. Although white rust is not a big concern, it is preferable to prevent it from spreading. No water should be kept or left in the musuinabe when not in use. To honor the name "musui" (means no water in Japanese), make a good habit of wiping and drying after each use.

Baking soda is often considered as a multipurpose cleaner but it does not work with aluminum. Discoloration caused by baking soda is hard to get rid of. Baking soda packaging itself carries a warning: "not to be used for aluminum products." Boiling "togijiru" (see Page 108) in the musuinabe before the first use prevents discoloration by allowing aluminum to form a protective film coating on the surface.

使いはじめ Before first use

鍋の本体と蓋に米のとぎ汁を入れ、10～15分ほど沸騰させる。これは黒変化防止のため。

Fill both the pot and lid with togijiru (milky water left over after washing uncooked rice). Let it boil for about 10-15 minutes. This prevents the pot and lid from blackening.

日々の手入れ Daily care

1 汚れが落ちやすくなるよう、余熱のあるうちに、スポンジに中性洗剤をつけて洗う。

To remove stuck on food easily, wash the pot while it is still warm using a mild detergent and a sponge.

2 水かぬるま湯で洗剤をすすぐ。

Rinse off the detergent with water or lukewarm water.

困ったときは Troubleshooting

焦げついたとき
Burned on food

1 鍋の余熱が残っているうちに、クレンザー（粉末状）を直接ふりかける。

While the pot is still warm, sprinkle a powder cleanser on the burnt on food.

3 布巾で拭いて水気を取る。

Wipe dry with a cloth.

2 ナイロンタワシかスチールウールのタワシで焦げをこすり落とし、水で洗い流す。

Scrub with a nylon scourer or steel wool. Rinse off the cleanser with water.

4 火にかけて完全に乾かしてしまう。これは水による白サビ防止のため。

Place the pot over heat to dry completely before putting it away. This prevents white rust caused by moisture.

やってはいけないこと
DON'TS

電子レンジ Microwave	食洗機 Dishwasher	重曹 Baking soda

和田助製作所の

ステンレスの鍋

Stainless Steel Saucepan / Wadasuke Seisakusho

電磁雪平鍋 24cm　Yukihira Nabe Induction Saucepan 24cm

素材 Materials	Nbステンレス、木 Nb Stainless steel, wood
サイズ Dimensions	直径24×高さ9.5cm D24 x H9.5cm
主な取扱い店 Stockists	和田助製作所オンラインショップ ニイミ洋食器店 Wadasuke Seisakusho Online Shop Niimi Yoshokkiten

その他のラインナップ
Product Information

電磁雪平鍋はほかに15cm、18cm、21cm、30cmがあり、計6サイズ。IHに使えるステンレスのしゃぶしゃぶ鍋やフライパン、ムール貝鍋もある。

The yukihira nabe induction saucepan comes in 6 sizes including 15cm, 18cm, 21cm and 30cm in diameter. Other induction products available include shabushabu hot pots, frying pans and mussel pots.

ステンレスを英語表記にすると Stainless。Stainとは「シミ」のこと。つまり、シミのない鋼のことをステンレススチールという。ただし、正確には「サビにくい」だ。サビにくい理由は鉄にクロムという金属を添加。クロムが酸素と結合してできる薄い保護膜がサビを防いでいるからだ。

ステンレスは、火を使わない道具は汚れもつきにくいため手間いらずだが、鍋は、強火で料理すると簡単に焦げる。しかし、研磨剤やタワシなどは遠慮なく使っていい。焦げがきつい場合は、重曹を使って磨けば大丈夫。ただし、ブラシなど磨くもので傷つけないように注意。「ヘアライン」と呼ばれる仕上げの磨き跡が残っていたら、その筋に沿って磨くときれいになる。

"Stainless" in stainless steel, strictly speaking, means "rust-less" not "rust-free". Stainless steel is more resistant to rust because it is made by adding chromium to iron. When chromium combines with oxygen, it forms a thin protective coating, which prevents rust.

Stainless steel utensils, especially the ones that are not used in contact with direct heat, are relatively care free. Stainless steel pots and pans on the other hand get burnt quite easily over high heat. The good news is that you can use abrasive cleaners and a tawashi or a scrubbing brush to clean. For stubborn stains, you can use baking soda. Just be mindful of scratching the surface. Marks from a hairline finish can be cleaned by polishing with the grain.

困ったときは Troubleshooting

焦げついたとき
Burnt on food

タワシにクレンザーをつけ、焦げた部分をこすって落とす。焦げがひどい場合は、重曹を使っても。

Put a powder cleanser on a tawashi or a scrubbing brush and scrub the burnt area. Baking soda can be used for stubborn stains.

油がついて黒く着色したとき
Burnt on grease

研磨効果のあるナイロンタワシなどでこすって落とす。

Scrub the burnt area with an abrasive nylon scrubber.

金属の道具

ステンレスの鍋

やってはいけないこと
DON'TS

| 電子レンジ
Microwave | 食洗機
Dishwasher |

水野正美の

銅の鍋

Copper Saucepan / Masami Mizuno

ミルクパン 小　Milk Pan small

素材 Material	銅 Copper
サイズ Dimensions	直径14×高さ6cm D14 x H6cm
主な取扱い店	Farmer's Table 夏至 THE SHOP 十二ヵ月 くるみの木cage
Stockists	Farmer's Table Geshi THE SHOP Jyunikagetsu Kuruminoki cage

その他のラインナップ　Product Information

ミルクパンはサイズ違いがあり、希望のサイズでの注文も可能。フライパ
ン、卵焼き器、スープパン、ドリップポット、カップ、楕円皿などもある。

The milk pan comes in various sizes and also available for made-to-order.
Other products available include frying pans, square frying pans, soup
pans, drip pots, cups and oval plates.

　一枚の板をどんどん叩いて、鍋のかたちにしていくのが「絞り」。板を紙
として想像するとわかるが、立体にするには皺を寄せる。叩きながらこの
皺を吸収していくのが「絞る」ことなのだ。熱を加え、組織をゆるめてから
叩き、金属を寄せていく。一気に急角度をつけると、皺が重なってしまい
割れてしまうので、何度にも分けて角度をつけていく、大変な作業だ。

　銅は酸化することで黒ずんだり、緑青（ろくしょう）（P137参照）が出ることがある。
これを事前に防ぐために、水野さんは鍋の内側に錫（すず）を引いている。この
錫は金属のへらなどで強くこすらない限りは落ちないが、経年変化で、だ
んだん薄くなっていく。取れてしまったら調理後は料理を速やかに器へ
移しておこう。また、錫の貼り直しもできる。銅には抗菌作用があり、雑菌
を退治し、さらに塩素（カルキ）を飛ばす効果もあり、ぬめりやにおいを
防ぐといわれている。水野さんは錫を引かないポットなども作っており、
一層銅の抗菌性が生かせ、水の味もまろやかだ。熱伝導が抜群で、かつ
均等にいき渡るため、銅のフライパンで作る卵焼きは大層うまくいく。

　金属は空焚きしたり、高温を加え続けると「なまる」ことがある。なまる
と組織がゆるみ、手でも曲がるほど柔らかくなってしまう。こうなったら
自分で直すのは不可能。作り手に戻して直してもらおう。

"Raising" is a metalworking process used to make a hollow form such
as a pot from a flat sheet of metal by repeated hammering. Like a piece
of paper a flat sheet of metal forms folds while taking shape and each
fold needs to be raised and closed by hammering. The metal is heated
up to loosen the molecular structure before the raising. Each fold needs
to be worked on in small sections because hammering at a sharp angle
too quickly will cause overlapping and increase the risk of crushing. The
raising is a time-consuming, painstaking process.

　Oxidation can cause discoloration (see Page 137) and verdigris patina
in copper. For prevention, Masami Mizuno lines his copperware with tin.
The tin does not come off unless scraped with something like a metallic
spatula but it will wear off over time. When the coating is worn away, it
is better to take food from the copper pot immediately after the cooking
is done. The tin can be replaced. Copper has disinfectant properties and
kills microbes. It also removes chlorine from water and prevents slime and
odor. Masami also makes untinned copper teapots and they maximize the
copper's disinfecting ability and make the water softer and taste better.
Copper is highly conductive and distributes heat evenly so cooking eggs
in copper frying pans works very well.

　Metal can be "weakened" when it is heated without water or exposed
to a high temperature for a long period of time. The molecular structure
becomes loose making it too soft and easily bent by hand. It is impossible
to fix copperware in this condition without professional help. It is
recommended to take to the maker for repair.

日々の手入れ Daily care

1 使用後はスポンジに中性洗剤をつ
けて洗う。

After use, wash the saucepan with a
mild detergent and a sponge.

2 水かぬるま湯で洗剤をすすぐ。

Rinse off the detergent with water or
lukewarm water.

3 布巾で拭いて水気を取る。

Wipe the saucepan with a cloth to dry.

長時間使わないとき Storage tips

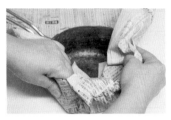

半年以上使わない場合は、酸化防止の
ために、新聞紙に包んでしまっておく。

If the saucepan is not going to be used for
six months or longer, wrap it in newspaper
before storing to prevent oxidation.

困ったときは Troubleshooting

焦げたとき
Burnt on food

1 水を入れて弱火にかけ、温まったら火を止めて1時間ほどおけば、焦げが浮いてくる。

Fill the saucepan with water and place it over low heat. When the water is warmed up, turn off the heat. Leave for about an hour, and the burnt on food will come off.

2 1で落ちなかった場合は、木べらなどを使ってこそげ落とす。

If this does not work, use a wooden spatula to scrape off the burnt food.

黒く着色したとき
Black stains

1 黒ズミは油。スチールウールのタワシにクレンザーをつける。

Black stains are burnt on grease. Put a powder cleanser on a steel wool pad.

2 1のタワシでゴシゴシとこすって黒ズミを落とし、水で洗い流す。

Scrub the stained area with the pad and rinse with water.

やってはいけないこと
DON'TS

電子レンジ Microwave	食洗機 Dishwasher	金属タワシ Metallic scrubber

銅の鍋の作り手を訪ねる

水野正美さん

Visiting Masami Mizuno / Maker of copper saucepans

　道具は使ってなんぼのもの。水野正美さんの作る鍋やポットは決して安くない。高価だと「もったいない」と、しまい込む人もいるが、水野さんの周りには使い込む人が多い。近所のパン屋さんの厨房では、使い込まれた水野さんのミルクパンを見つけた。別のコーヒー屋さんは、水野さん作のドリップポットを日々定点観測して、一日何百杯もコーヒーを淹れながら、ポットが変化していく様を記録している。もちろん、水野さん自身も愛用者だ。自宅の鍋すべてが自作の銅鍋で、どれもよく使い込まれているのがわかる。

　銅製のものは、使い込むほどいい風合いになっていく。だがはじめは、「銅はフライパンに適さないと思い込んでいた」と水野さんは話す。お客さんに言われて、作ってみた。自分で使ってみると、「鉄は火が熱源に集中しますが、銅は熱伝導がいいので全体にいき渡ったんですよ」。以来、フライパンも水野さんの重要なアイテムとなった。

「この鍋やポットは、確実に自分より長生きしますからね」。作業は果てしないように感じられたが、この思いがあれば、一個に何万回でも金槌をあてられるのだろう。

The true value of a tool is in its use. The pots and kettles Masami Mizuno makes are not cheap by any means. Some people store away expensive items because they are "too good" for everyday use but Masami has a few neighbors who use them on daily basis. I found a well-used milk pan made by Masami in a baker's kitchen in his neighborhood. A coffee shop owner nearby his house monitors on his drip coffee pot, also made by Masami, every day. He keeps records on how his pot changes its color while serving several hundred cups of coffee a day. Masami himself, as well expected, is a regular user of copperware. The pots at his house are all copper and made by him and it is easy to see that each of them is well-used.

　The texture of copperware improves as you use it. Masami confides that he "used to assume that copper was not a good material for making frying pans." But that changed when one of his customers asked him to make one. So Masami made one and tested out by himself. That was when he discovered that "with iron, heat concentrates of its source, but copper allows it to spread evenly because it has great conductivity." Frying pans have been an important item for Masami ever since.

　"These pots and kettles will live on long after I am gone," says Masami. Creating handcrafted copperware seems like a job that never ends, but with his tireless spirit, Masami appears to be able to keep making tens of thousands of hammer strokes to make a single pot.

1.平らな銅板から立体が生まれる。「ヒダをたくし上げながら絞る」作業を細かくすることで、立ち上がってくる。2_3.「なます」作業。バーナーを当てて真っ黒になっているが、この作業で組織を緩めている。叩く前には必ずこの作業をする。

1.A solid shape is created from a flat copper sheet. By "raising and tucking up folds" in small sections at a time, the sheet starts to rise up. 2_3."Annealing" process. The pot has been blackened using a hand burner. This process loosens the molecular structure of the copper and is carried out before any hammering work.

1.水野さんの家で毎日使われている鍋や
ポット。「どれも、僕より確実に長生きする
からね」と水野さん。2.焦げも愛嬌。気に
なるならば、スチールウールタワシできれい
にする。

1.The pots and pans used every day at
Masami's home. "Each of them will live on
long after I am gone," says Masami. 2.Burnt
stains are part of the charm. But, if not
wanted, they can be removed by scrubbing
with a steel wool scourer.

作り手の使い方

1.銅のフライパンは、全体が平均して温まるため、スクランブルエッグなどの卵料理がおいしくできる。後ろにケトルが置いてあるが、油が飛んだら拭かないと焦げなどの原因になる。
2.水野さんが作ってくれたこの日の昼食は、野菜炒めとスクランブルエッグ。真鍮(写真右)と銅のお皿にご飯も一緒に盛りつけてワンプレートに。金属の皿はあまり想像がつかなかったが、食材の色映りがいい。

How the makers use it

1.The copper frying pan allows heat to spread evenly and is good for cooking eggs. The kettle left on the stove at the back is at risk of getting burnt stains from cooking oils unless it is wiped off immediately. 2.Stir-fry vegetables and scrambled eggs Masami cooked us for lunch. They are served with rice as a one-plate dish on a brass plate (on the right) and copper plates. I had not thought of using metal plates for serving food before, but they actually highlight the food colors.

野田琺瑯の

琺瑯の鍋

Enamel Pot / Noda Horo

NOMAKUキャセロール 20cm　Nomaku Casserole 20cm

素材 Material	琺瑯 Enamel
サイズ Dimensions	直径20.7×高さ14.5cm D20.7 x H14.5cm
主な取扱い店 Stockist	野田琺瑯に問い合わせを Please contact Noda Horo

その他のラインナップ Product Information

NOMAKUシリーズは少量生産のため、在庫は要確認。ほかに、保存容器、ケトル・ポット、調理小物など多数のアイテムが揃う。

The NOMAKU series of cookware is produced in low volumes. Please check the store for stock. Many other products are available including storage containers, kettle pots and cooking utensils.

鉄にガラスを焼きつけているのが琺瑯。サビやすいけれど強い鉄と、衛生的で美しいが壊れやすいガラスの融合したものだ。琺瑯は丈夫な素材といわれるが、ガラス質の部分は欠けやすい。かくいう私も、ポットの蓋はすぐに落として欠けさせてしまった。軽い衝撃だったので黒色が見えているが、この黒い部分はガラス質なのでサビることはない。しかし、強く落として、鈍いシルバー色が見えたら、それは鉄が露出したことになる。こういう風に欠けたところは、油をつけてサビを防ぐのも一手。塩分がこびりついたままにはしないことだ。鉄が露出した部分が鍋の内側ならば、ぬか漬けを漬ける容器にするのもおすすめ。ぬか床に釘を入れるのは、漬け物のナスを色良くしたり、鉄分を摂るために行うこと。欠けて鉄が見える琺瑯もこれと同じ働きをすることになるのだ。

野田琺瑯に嫁いで45年の野田善子さんは、琺瑯の一番の愛用者。「琺瑯は、食材や料理の風味を変化させにくいうえ、汚れが落としやすく、細菌の繁殖を防ぎます。直火にかけられるので保存容器でもそのまま調理ができ、器として食卓にも出せます」と善子さんの話を聞いていると、鍋だけでなく保存容器も使いたくなってくる。

Vitreous enamel is made by fusing melted glass particles to metal by firing at high temperatures. Enamel cookware is a combination of steel that is durable but rusts easily, and glass that is beautiful and hygienic but liable to break. Enamel is thought to be tough and sturdy as a material but it is prone to chipping because of its glass properties. I am certainly not one of the careful owners. My enamel pot lid has a chip because I dropped it soon after I purchased it. Luckily the impact was small, only revealing black glaze which was glass so I did not need to worry about rust. If it was dropped on a hard surface and dull silver color appear, that is the steel underneath. One way to prevent rust on the chipped area is to coat it with oil. Burnt on salty foods on the chipped area should not be left as this also causes rust. If your enamel pot has exposed steel inside, you can use it as a container for making "nukazuke" (Japanese rice bran pickles). It is an old practice in Japan to keep nails in a nukazuke container because iron in nails brightens vegetable colors, an eggplant for example. There is also a health benefit in taking iron from the nails. An enamel pot with exposed steel has the same effect.

Yoshiko Noda married into the Noda family (Noda Horo) 45 years ago and adores enamelware. "Enamel is excellent in retaining the flavor of foods and easy to clean. It prevents the growth of bacteria. It is flameproof and you can even use an enamel storage canister to cook on a stove. What's more, it is pretty enough to serve on the table." Listening to her made me want to use not only enamel pots but canisters as well in my kitchen.

日々の手入れ Daily care

1 使用後はスポンジに中性洗剤をつけて洗う。

After use, wash the pot with a mild detergent and a sponge.

2 水かぬるま湯で洗剤をすすぐ。

Rinse off the detergent with water or lukewarm water.

3 布巾で拭いて水気を取ってからしまう。

Wipe the pot with a cloth to dry before putting it away.

特別な手入れ Occasional care

サビ防止に
Rust prevention

フチや欠けた部分などのサビ防止には、食用油（何でもOK）を塗るといい。

Coat the rim and chipped edges with cooking oil (any kind) to prevent them from rusting.

やってはいけないこと
DON'TS

電子レンジ Microwave	食洗機 Dishwasher	金属タワシ Metallic scrubber

金属タワシ、クレンザーは表面を傷つけるので使わない。
Do not use abrasive cleansers or a metallic washing brush as they will scratch the surface.

困ったときは Troubleshooting

焦げたとき
Burnt on food

1 焦がした鍋にぬるま湯を入れ、そこに大さじ1の重曹を入れる。

Fill the burnt pot with lukewarm water and add one tablespoon of baking soda.

4 3の状態で半日〜1日おくと焦げが浮いてくる。

Leave for a half day or whole day, and the burnt on food will come off.

2 1に食用油（何でもOK）を少量（2〜3滴）入れる。

Add 2-3 drops of cooking oil (any kind) to the pot.

5 4の水を捨ててスポンジに中性洗剤をつけて洗う。焦げがひどいときは、1〜5を何度か繰り返す。

Discard the water and wash the pot with a mild detergent and a sponge. For stubborn stains, repeat the process 1-5 several times.

3 火にかけ、沸騰したら止める。

Place the pot over heat. Bring to a boil and turn off the heat.

omoto 鈴木康人の
鋼<ruby>はがね</ruby>の包丁

Hagane Hocho Knife (carbon steel knife) / omoto Yasuto Suzuki

菜切り包丁	Nakiri (vegetable) Hocho Knife
素材 Materials	鉄、鋼、木 Iron, Carbon steel, Wood
サイズ Dimensions	刃の部分：長さ16×幅5cm Blade: L16 x W5cm
主な取扱い店 Stockists	かぐれ表参道店 jokogumo Kagure Omotesando jokogumo

その他のラインナップ Product Information
刺身包丁、ペティナイフなどもある。展示会ではおすすめの
メーカーの砥石も販売している。

Other knives available include sashimi hocho knives and
paring knives. Recommended sharpening stones are sold at
fairs and exhibitions in which Yasuto Suzuki participates.

　金属を薄くしたら切れる訳ではない。切るためには「鋼」が必要だ。ここでいう鋼は「刃金」といって、刃物の刃先に用いる金属のこと。鉄に鋼がついているものと、鋼のみでできているものもある。鋼には堅さと粘りがあり、この2つは包丁にたる重要なポイントだ。鋼は約800度に加熱してから急冷する「焼き入れ」で堅くなり、180度ぐらいに再加熱する「焼き戻し」で粘り強さが出るのだ。

　包丁には和包丁と洋包丁がある。和包丁は鉄と鋼の打刃物で、出刃、刺身、菜切りなど、素人でもすぐに数種類の包丁名をいえるほど、種類は多い。これは、和食においては食材を美しく見せることに重点を置いたため。昨今は、これらの機能を集約した三徳包丁一本で済ませる人も多い。一方、洋包丁は鋼の刃のものが多いが、家庭用の種類は少なく、調理の効率重視で、牛刀とペティナイフ程度でどんな食材でも切れる。

　サビが怖くて、鉄の包丁を敬遠する人はステンレス（P111参照）を使っているだろう。だが、ステンレスといっても、サビは出る。洗いはしっかりしたほうがいい。また、ステンレスでも研ぐとしっかり切れるようになる。

Making a piece of metal thinner does not mean it can cut things. To be able to cut, it needs "hagane" or steel. The word "hagane" in Japanese refers to the steel used for knife blades. Some knives are made by forging hagane with iron and others are made of hagane alone. Sharpness and resilience are the two important qualities for hagane to make a good hocho knife. The steel is heated to 800 degrees first and placed in water for rapid cooling. This process is called "yakiire" or "quenching" and hardens the steel. The steel is heated again at a lower temperature at 180 degrees for "yakimodoshi" or tempering to gain resilience.

　There are Japanese kitchen knives and Western kitchen knives. Traditional Japanese kitchen knives are made by forging iron and hagane and there are so many varieties that even amateur chefs can only name a few: deba (for cutting fish and meat), sashimi (for filleting fish) and nakiri (for cutting vegetables). This is because food presentation has been highly emphasized in traditional Japanese cuisine, making ingredients visually appealing. Nowadays santoku knives are popular with many people for their ability to cut meat, fish and vegetables (Santoku means "three virtues"). The Western style knives have a smaller range for household use. There is more focus on cooking efficiency and gyutou or chef's knives and paring knives are sufficient to cut any ingredients.

　Those who shy away from steel kitchen knives because of rust problems would probably choose stainless steel knives (see Page 111). But stainless steel knives can still get rusty. Thorough washing after every use is important and sharpening is also beneficial.

使いはじめ Before first use

1 包丁の手入れをずっと行うことを考えると、荒砥（♯120〜600）、中砥（♯1000前後）、仕上げ用（♯3000〜）の3種類の砥石が必要なので買い揃えるといい。

To properly care for the hocho knife and to keep it in good condition for a long period time, it is recommended to use three types sharpening stones with different grits: a coarse stone (120-600 grit), a medium stone (around 1000 grit) and a finishing stone (3000+ grit).

2 はじめて使うときは、仕上げ用の砥石で軽く研ぎ、「本刃」をつける*。

Before using the knife for the first time, sharpen the blade lightly on the finishing stone. This process is called "honbazuke", blade-honing.

※一般的に店で販売される包丁のほとんどは本刃がついているが、鈍角の刃つけがされている場合もある。鈍角な刃でも切れるが、使う前に研いで「本刃」をつける。買う際に本刃がついているかどうかを確認しよう。

＊Most hocho knives sold in stores come with honbazuke finish but some do not and need this initial sharpening. It is best to check at the store before purchase.

日々の手入れ Daily care

1 使用後はスポンジに中性洗剤をつけ、刃に気をつけながら洗う。

After use, wash the hocho knife with a mild detergent and a sponge. Be careful of the blade.

2 水かぬるま湯で洗剤をすすいだら、布巾で拭いて水気をしっかり取る。

Rinse off the detergent with water or lukewarm water and dry thoroughly with a cloth.

3 使用頻度にもよるが、1週間に1回くらいは仕上げ用の砥石で研ぐ。

Although the frequency of sharpening depends on how often the knife is used, weekly sharpening with the finishing stone is recommended.

困ったときは Troubleshooting

切れ味が悪くなったとき
Blunt edges

1 砥石は使っていると真ん中がへこんでくるため、砥石どうしをこすり合わせて平らにする。研ぐ前に砥石は水に浸し、水をたっぷり吸わせておく。研ぐときは、砥石の下に濡れ布巾を置くなどして、砥石が動かないように安定させる。合成砥石は種類によって水に浸して使うものと、長時間水に浸さないように注意するものがある。

The center of the sharpening stone wears off with use and becomes uneven. To flatten the surface, take another sharpening stone and grind the two stones against each other. Soak the stones in water before use. When sharpening the knife, lay a damp cloth under the bottom stone to prevent it from slipping. Some synthetic stones need soaking before use while others shoud not be soaked for a long time.

2 砥石に包丁をあて、一定の角度を保ち、手前から奥に向かって研ぐ。手前の位置に戻すときは力を弱めるか、完全に浮かせてもOK。

Place the hocho knife on the sharpening stone. Holding the knife at an angle, apply some pressure on the blade and push the knife away from your body. When pulling the knife back, apply less pressure or lift the knife from the stone.

3 刃のつけ根から先端に向かって、2を何回か繰り返す。途中、砥石の水分がなくならないよう、砥石に水をかけながら行う。

Repeat step 2 several times starting from the base of the blade and to the tip. Keep applying water on the stone while sharpening.

4 刃のミネのほうから刃先に向けて指でさわり、刃先がざらついていたら研げている証拠。包丁を裏返し、反対の面も同様にして研ぐ。荒砥の砥石からはじめて中砥、仕上げ用の順番に砥石を変え、2〜4の要領で研いでいく。

Run fingertips from the spine of the knife towards the edge. When the edge feels rough to the fingertips, it is done. Turn the knife over and work on the other side of the blade. Do the sharpening process above three times. Use the coarse stone the first time, then the medium stone and the finishing stone for the final time.

困ったときは Troubleshooting

サビが出たとき
Rust

1 サビの部分をスチールウールのタワシでこすって落とす。

Scrub off the rust with steel wool.

2 あるいは水につけたサンドペーパー（＃600程度）をかけてもサビは落ちる。

Sanding with wet sandpaper (around 600 grit) is also effective to remove the rust.

長時間使わないとき Storage tips

1 しばらく使わないときは、椿油かオリーブオイルをキッチンペーパーに染み込ませ、刃の両面に塗る。

If the hocho knife is not going to be used for a while, wipe both sides of the blade with a paper towel dipped in tsubaki abura (camellia oil) or olive oil.

2 新聞紙に包んでしまう。

Wrap the knife in newspaper and store.

やってはいけないこと
DON'TS

電子レンジ	食洗機	金属タワシ	天日干し
Microwave	Dishwasher	Metallic scrubber	Dry in direct sunlight

包丁を火であぶってはいけない。
Do not dry the hocho knife over direct flame.

洗う道具の話
Washing Tools

　洗う道具にこだわりを持つ人は多いだろう。私は圧倒的にタワシ派だ。棕櫚という温暖な地域に生育する木の樹皮を使ったものだ。タワシというとトゲトゲして痛そうと思うだろうが、国産の棕櫚は柔らかく、強く握っても痛くない。これで、鉄のフライパンも白木のおひつ、弁当箱も洗う。タワシがないと落ち着かない。もうひとつが綿を編んだもの。本書では使用していないが、これはきちんとした漆器を扱う店が、漆用に売っているものだ。編み方がいいのか、漆に優しく持ちもいい。これでなくても、漆には天然繊維をおすすめする。

Many of us have our favorite washing tool. My favorite is definitely tawashi. Tawashi is made from the bark of hemp palm trees, which grow in temperate regions. Despite its rough and bristly look, the Japanese hemp palm tawashi is soft to touch and does not hurt when you grip it. I use my tawashi to clean my iron frying pan, wooden ohitsu (a container for cooked rice) and lunch box. I feel awkward without a tawashi in my kitchen. There is another good washing cloth made of knitted cotton although it is not used in this book. It is made especially for urushi lacquerware and sold at urushi ware stores. Perhaps because of the way it is knitted, the cloth is gentle on urushi and very durable. If this type of washing cloth is unavailable, a wash cloth made from natural fiber is recommended to use with urushi ware.

本書で使用した主な洗う道具
Main washing tools mentioned in this book

スポンジ Sponge

タワシ（棕櫚）Tawashi (shuro, hemp palm)

金属タワシ Metallic scourer

スチールウールのタワシ Steel wool

TAjiKAの

ステンレスの
キッチンばさみ

Stainless Steel Kitchen Shears / TAjiKA

KITCHEN SHEARS

素材 Material	ハイカーボンステンレス High carbon stainless steel
サイズ Dimension	長さ20.5㎝（手作りのため多少の差が出る） L 20.5㎝ (because the shears are hand-made, the size will vary slightly)
主な取扱い店	松屋銀座デザインコレクション くらすこと Gloini Analogue life まちのシューレ963
Stockists	Matsuya Ginza Design Collection Kurasukoto Gloini Analogue life Machino-schule 963

その他のラインナップ Product Information
KITCHEN SHEARSには一体型とセパレートタイプがあり、この写真のはさみは一体型。ほかに、branch & root shears、garden cripper、HOUSEHOLD SCISSORS、FLOWER SHEARSなどもある。

KITCHEN SHEARS are available in separable and non-separable types. The shears shown in the photograph are non-separable. Other products available include branch & root shears, garden clippers, HOUSEHOLD SCISSORS, and FLOWER SHEARS.

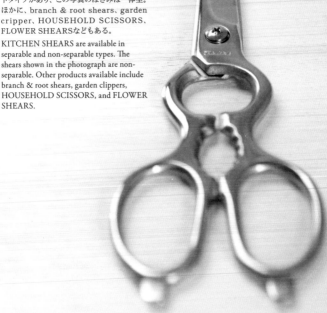

TAjiKAは、多鹿治夫鋏製作所という洋裁ばさみを専門に作っている工房が、より多くの人にはさみのことを知ってもらいたいと作ったブランド。包丁は刃1枚だが、はさみは2枚の刃を重ねて切る。子どもの頃、はさみの2枚の刃の間に紙を滑らせてしまい、なかなか切れずに悔しかったことを思い出す。つまり、はさみとは使いこなさなければならないもの。道具としてはかなり高等なものなのだ。

キッチンばさみでは、紙やビニールなどの包装だけでなく、野菜や肉などの食材も切る。切る対象物に幅がある上、食材に刃が触れてしまうのだから、洗わなければならない。まな板に色やにおいをつけたくないものや、肉でまな板を汚したくないときなどは、キッチンばさみで切りたくなる。こんなふうに使うには、やはり扱いやすくてサビにくいステンレスがいい。

刃の一体型に対してセパレートタイプは分解できるので、研げるのではと思い、研ぎ方を教えて欲しいと伝えると「お客さんは研がずに送ってください」と、多鹿大輔さんに即答された。刃物の調整はあくまでプロの仕事。「素人は研げないものなので、サビないように、日々気をつけてもらいたい」というのが作り手の願いだ。ステンレスなのでサビは出にくいが、塩分の多い食材を切ってそのままにしたらサビる可能性大。あとで後悔しないように、きちんと洗い、しっかり拭くという癖をつけておきたいものだ。

Tajika Haruo Hasami Seisakusho is a maker of scissors and shears and TAjiKa is their newer brand with the objective of making quality scissors more accessible to general consumers. Unlike knives, scissors consist of two blades that are set up to meet each other to cut thin materials. My childhood memory of scissors is a frustrating one. I tried to cut a piece of paper but it kept slipping between the two blades. Scissors are sophisticated tools and it takes practice to use them properly and efficiently.

Kitchen scissors are used for cutting a wide range of items, from paper and plastic wrappings to vegetables and meat, so they require frequent washing to stay clean. They are preferred to knives to stop food stains, odors and bacteria in raw meat getting onto cutting boards. To meet the demands of these multiple uses, the best material for kitchen scissors is stainless steel that is easy to handle and resistant to rust.

Once I had a pair of separable scissors and wanted to sharpen the blades by myself. When I made an enquiry to Daisuke Tajika from Tajika Haruo ironworks about how to sharpen them, I got an instant, short response. "We ask our customers not to sharpen them but just send to us." I realized that fixing problems with edged tools is a matter for professionals. "The blades cannot be sharpened properly by amateurs. We just want our customers to look after their scissors to prevent rust," is the request from the maker. Although they are rust-resistant, stainless steel scissors can get rusty if not cleaned after cutting salt-rich food. For prevention, it is a good idea to make a habit of thoroughly washing and wiping your kitchen scissors after each use.

一体型の場合　Non-separable type shears

日々の手入れ Daily care

1 使用後はスポンジに中性洗剤をつけ、まずは刃先から洗う。

After use, wash the shears with a mild detergent and a sponge. Start with the points.

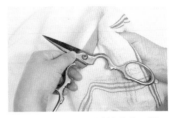

4 水かぬるま湯で洗剤をすすいだら、布巾で刃先から拭く。

Rinse off the detergent with water or lukewarm water. Wipe the shears with a cloth, starting with the points.

2 刃と刃が重なる部分のネジ下なども丁寧に洗う。

Wash the overlapping area thoroughly as well.

5 ネジ下の部分も水気が残らないように丁寧に拭く。

Wipe under the screw thoroughly so that no moisture is left.

3 刃を閉じて全体を洗う。裏側も1〜3と同様にして洗う。

Close the shears and wash them all over. Wash the other side, repeating the steps above.

特別な手入れ Occasional care

切れ味を保つために
Keeping the shears sharp

1 水気や汚れなどを取り除くために、布巾で丁寧に乾拭きする。

Wipe the shears thoroughly with a dry cloth to remove moisture and dirt.

2 キッチンペーパーにオリーブオイルや椿油などを少量染み込ませ、刃に塗る。

Add a small amount of tsubaki abura (camellia oil) or olive oil to a paper towel to lubricate the blades.

3 ネジ下に適度な油分があると開閉が滑らかになる。また、油は膜を作ることでサビ防止にもなる。

Oiling under the screw helps the blades move more smoothly. A thin coat of oil also prevents the shears from rusting.

注意すること Special attention

分解できるセパレートタイプは、使っているとたまにネジがゆるむことがあるが、自分で締めると、刃の噛み合わせが狂う可能性がある。調整は必ず作り手に任せること。

The screw on separable shears can become loose. If it happens, take them to the maker for adjustment instead of trying to fix by yourself. If not handled carefully, the blades might end up not meeting properly.

やってはいけないこと
DON'TS

電子レンジ Microwave　天日干し Dry in direct sunlight

ラッキーウッドの

シルバーのカトラリー

Silver Cutlery / LUCKYWOOD

〈シルバーレーク〉シリーズ <Silver Lake> Series

素材 Materials	ニッケルシルバー、銀メッキ Nickel silver, silver plate
サイズ	テーブルフォーク：長さ19.9㎝ デザートスプーン：長さ18.7㎝ スープスプーン：長さ17.7㎝
Sizes	Table Fork: L19.9cm Desert Spoon: L18.7cm Soup Spoon: L17.7cm
主な取扱い店	ニイミ洋食器店 全国の有名百貨店・専門店
Stockists	Niimi Yoshokkiten Leading Department Stores and Specialty Stores in Japan

その他のラインナップ Product Information
サイズ、種類は多数ある。
The products are available in a variety of types and sizes.

　西洋アンティークの世界では使い込まれた銀器の方が、同じものの新品より高値で取引されることがあるそうだ。変色は銀とは切っても切れないもの。それを楽しむのが銀製品だ。専用の銀磨きを使うと、驚くほどきれいになる。だが、それは最小限にとどめて、毎日布で拭いて、自然な輝きを楽しむのがおすすめだ。

　鉄に赤サビを発生させる酸化は、金属を劣化させる原因だが、銀は酸素以外のものとも化合しやすく、塩化も硫化もある。これを防ぐには、空気、湿気、日光を遮断、というなんとも過保護な状態にしなくてはいけないのだが、それよりも何よりも「使って拭くのが一番」なのだ。ガスコンロは硫黄分を出すため、近くに置いておくと銀が変色しやすい。そのために近くには置かない方がいい。同じ理由で、卵やゴムも変色する元となる。

　洗うときは、手洗い用の食器用洗剤を使うこと。重曹も変色を取ることができる（よく洗浄すること）。「多少の汚れなら、柔らかい布でびっくりするほど簡単に落ちます。銀磨きを使うと、元のミラー色に戻ってしまうからもったいないですよ」と言われた。漆（P37参照）でも書いた「新品に戻ってしまってもったいない」。この言葉はシルバーにも当てはまる。焼物の貫入のように、金属も使い込んでいく素材なのだ。

In the antique business in the Western countries, well-used silverware is sometimes traded at a higher price than its brand-new counterpart. Discoloration is inevitable in silverware and it is part of pleasure of ownership to see these changes. Cleaning with silver polish can restore the original mirror shine, but I recommend daily wiping by hand to enjoy the natural shine and keep the use of silver polish to a minimum.

　Oxidation causes rust in iron and deterioration in metals. Silver also combines with other chemical elements besides oxygen such as chloride and sulfur. To protect silverware from chemical reactions, it needs to be closed off from air, moisture and sunlight. But instead of being so over-protective, it would be more enjoyable to use it and then clean it. The silverware should be kept away from gas stove, eggs and plastic rubbers because they all contain sulfur and cause discoloration in silver.

　For washing, use a dish-washing detergent. Baking soda can also be used to remove the discoloration but needs thorough rinsing. I was told that "most dirt and marks can be easily removed by wiping with a soft cloth. If you use a silver polish, a mirror shine will be back, but that will be a shame." The words "it will be a shame to bring back to brand-new condition" were mentioned earlier about urushi lacquer (see Page 37) and the same can be said of silver. Like kan-nyuu in ceramics, metal ware develops its character with use.

日々の手入れ Daily care

1 使用後はスポンジに中性洗剤をつ
けて洗う。

After use, wash the cutlery with a mild
detergent and a sponge.

2 水かぬるま湯で洗剤をすすいだら、
布巾で拭く。

Rinse off the detergent with water or
lukewarm water and wipe with a cloth
to dry.

3 数日使わなかったら、きれいな布
で乾拭きすると、変色しにくくなる。

When the cutlery has not been used
for a few days, buff with a clean cloth
to prevent tarnish.

困ったときは Troubleshooting

変色したとき
Tarnish

1 ゴム手袋をつけ、市販の銀磨き液
を布に染み込ませて磨く。

Wear rubber gloves and polish the
cutlery with a cloth dipped in a silver
polishing liquid available at stores.

2 水かぬるま湯でしっかりとすすぎ、
布巾で拭いて水気を取る。

Rinse thoroughly with water or
lukewarm water and wipe with a cloth
to dry.

やってはいけないこと
DON'TS

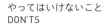

| 電子レンジ Microwave | 食洗機 Dishwasher | 金属タワシ Metallic scrubber | 天日干し Dry in direct sunlight |

column

金属が変化しても驚かないように。**1.**鉄は酸化で赤サビができる。**2.**銀は硫黄分に反応し硫化が起きて黒ずむ。**3.**アルミはアルカリに反応して黒くなる黒変化を起こす。**4.**銅が酸化すると緑青ができる。

Do not be surprised with reactions of metals. **1.**Iron rusts by oxidation. **2.**Silver becomes darker when it reacts with sulfur. **3.**Aluminum becomes discolored when it reacts with alkaline. **4.**When copper is oxidized, verdigris patina forms.

金属の道具の変化
Reactions of Metals

　金属は放っておくとその素材が自然界の構成要素と反応する。素材によって、何に反応するかが違い、さらに反応の仕方が違うから難しい。

　たとえば鉄の赤サビ。「赤サビは無害」というが「一般的にいわれる鉄の赤サビである酸化鉄（III）は無毒だが、それが本当に酸化鉄かどうかは、調べないとわからない」。ちなみに、写真1は私物。中は真っ赤だが沸かしたお湯は透明。水質もいいのでそのまま愛用している。写真4は私物のおろし金。銅の緑青は日本画の顔料にもなり、当然無害だ。だが、無害と無味は別物。味にも関わりがあるので、歯ブラシで緑青を落として使っている。

When metals are left untreated, they react with elements present in the atmosphere. What each metal reacts with and how it reacts depends on elements and that makes handling of metals a little tricky.

　Rust on iron, for example, is said to be "harmless". The problem is that "although iron (III) oxide,commonly known as red rust on iron, is non-toxic, we do not know if the chemical compound present is really iron oxide or not unless we check it out." Photograph 1 is my iron kettle. The inside is bright red, but the hot water I boil in it is transparent. Because the quality of the water is good, I am using the kettle as it is. Photograph 4 is my grater. Verdigris patina on copper is harmless and used as pigment for Nihonga (Japanese-style painting). Harmless to the body does not mean harmless to flavor however. Patina does affect the flavor of food, so I remove it from my grater with a toothbrush before use.

本書で紹介した台所道具の作り手の問い合わせ先
Contact details for the makers

名前に＊印がついている人は、販売もしています。
以下に明記していない作り手の作品は、取扱い店へお問い合わせください。

The makers with the ＊ symbol sell their products directly to customers.
For products by makers whose details are not included below, please contact their stockists.

川端健夫 / Takeo Kawabata ＊
滋賀県甲賀市甲南町野川835
835 Nogawa, Konancho, Koka, Shiga
TEL0748-86-1552
http://mammamia-project.jp/

木屋 / Kiya ＊
東京都中央区日本橋室町2-2-1コレド室町1F
COREDO Muromachi1F 2-2-1
Nihonbashimuromachi, Chuo-ku,Tokyo
TEL03-3241-0110
http://www.kiya-hamono.co.jp/

**柴田慶信商店 /
Shibata Yoshinobu Shoten ＊**
秋田県大館市御成町2-15-28
2-15-28 Onaricho, Odate, Akita
TEL0186-42-6123
http://magewappa.com/

照宝 / Shouhou ＊
神奈川県横浜市中区山下町150
150 Yamashitacho, Yokohama Naka-ku,
Kanagawa
TEL045-681-0234
http://www.shouhou.jp/

**ゆかい社中そらぐみ /
Yukaishachu Soragumi ＊**
徳島県徳島市新浜町4-1-39-2F
2F 4-1-39 Shinhamacho, Tokushima, Tokushima
TEL090-2895-3974
http://sora-dougu.jugem.jp

滴生舎 / Tekiseisha ＊
岩手県二戸市浄法寺町御山中前田23-6
23-6 Onyamanakamaeta, Jobojimachi, Ninohe,
Iwate
TEL0195-38-2511
http://www.tekiseisha.com/

喜八工房 / Kihachi Kobo ＊
石川県加賀市山中温泉塚谷町イ323
i323 Yamanakaonsen, Tsukatanimachi, Kaga,
Ishikawa
TEL0761-78-0048
http://www.kihachi-web.com/

久保一幸 / Kazuyuki Kubo＊
http://www.geocities.jp/iccouikkou/

**安藤雅信（ギャルリももぐさ）/
Masanobu Ando (Galerie Momogusa) ＊**
岐阜県多治見市東栄町2-8-16
2-8-16 Toeicho, Tajimi, Gifu
TEL0572-21-3368
http://www.momogusa.jp/

**山本忠正（やまほん陶房）/
Tadamasa Yamamoto(Yamahon Tobo)**
三重県伊賀市丸柱2053
2053 Marubashira, Iga, Mie
TEL0595-44-1600

一陽窯 / Ichiyougama ＊
岡山県備前市伊部670
670 Inbe, Bizen, Okayama
TEL0869-64-3655
https://www.facebook.com/ichiyougama

成田理俊 / Takayoshi Narita
http://studiotint.exblog.jp/

及源鋳造 / Oigen Foundry ＊
岩手県奥州市水沢区羽田町字堀ノ内45
45 Horinouchi, Hadacho, Mizusawa-ku, Osyu,
Iwate
TEL0197-24-2411
http://oigen.jp/

山田工業所 / Yamada Kogyosho
http://www.yamadanabe.com/

生活春秋 / Seikatsu Shunju ＊
http://www.musui.co.jp/

和田助製作所 / Wadasuke Seisakusho ＊
http://www.wadasuke.co.jp/

水野正美 / Masami Mizuno
https://sites.google.com/site/mizuno033/

野田琺瑯 / Noda Horo
http://www.nodahoro.com/

omoto 鈴木康人 / omoto Yasuto Suzuki
http://www.nunototetsu.com/

TAjiKA
http://www.tajikahasami.com/

ラッキーウッド / LUCKYWOOD
https://www.luckywood.jp/

取扱い店リスト

Stockists list

紹介している商品の取扱い店舗でも、売り切れだったり、常に取扱っているとは限りません。
また、サイズなども変更になることがありますので、店舗で確認するようにしてください。

The products introduced in this book may be sold out or not be always available at their stockists.
Sizes and other information are subject to change. Please check at the store.

川端健夫の 白木の器
Shiraki Unvarnished Woodenware /
Takeo Kawabata

ギャラリー・マンマミーア /
gallery-mamma mia
滋賀県甲賀市甲南町野川835
835 Nogawa, Konancho, Koka, Shiga
TEL0748-86-1552
http://mammamia-project.jp/

KOHORO
東京都世田谷区玉川3-12-11-1F
1F 3-12-11 Tamagawa, Setagaya-ku, Tokyo
TEL03-5717-9401
http://www.kohoro.jp/

スパイラルマーケット / Spiral Market
東京都港区南青山5-6-23スパイラル2F
Spiral2F 5-6-23 Minamiaoyama, Minato-ku,
Tokyo
TEL03-3498-5792
http://www.spiral.co.jp/shop_restaurant/spiral_
market/

CLASKA Gallery & Shop "DO" 日本橋店 /
CLASKA Gallery & Shop "DO" Nihonbashi
東京都中央区日本橋室町1-5-5コレド室町3 2F
COREDO Muromachi3 2F 1-5-5
Nihonbashimuromachi, Chuo-ku, Tokyo
TEL03-6262-3270
http://do.claska.com

木屋のまな板
Manaita Cutting Board / Kiya

日本橋 木屋本店 / Kiya Nihonbashi Main Store
東京都中央区日本橋室町2-2-1コレド室町1F
COREDO Muromachi 1F 2-2-1
Nihonbashimuromachi, Chuo-ku, Tokyo
TEL03-3241-0110
http://www.kiya-hamono.co.jp/

木屋玉川店 / Kiya Tamagawa
TEL03-3707-2776

木屋大丸梅田店 / Kiya Daimaru Umeda
TEL06-6342-9510

木屋東武池袋店 / Kiya Tobu Ikebukuro
TEL03-5951-2551

木屋博多大丸福岡天神店 /
Kiya Hakata Daimaru Fukuoka Tenjin
TEL092-714-0323

木屋大丸東京店 / Kiya Daimaru Tokyo
TEL03-6895-2562

柴田慶信商店の曲げわっぱ
Magewappa (bentwood ware) /
Shibata Yoshinobu Shoten

柴田慶信商店 本店 /
Shibata Yoshinobu Shoten Main Store
秋田県大館市御成町2-15-28
2-15-28 Onaricho, Odate, Akita
TEL0186-42-6123
http://magewappa.com/

柴田慶信商店 浅草店 /
Shibata Yoshinobu Shoten Asakusa
東京都台東区雷門1-13-10
1-13-10 Kaminarimon, Taito-ku, Tokyo
TEL03-6231-6477

POST DETAIL
東京都渋谷区千駄ケ谷3-51-5
3-51-5 Sendagaya, Shibuya-ku, Tokyo
TEL03-3402-5355
http://www.postdetail.com/

Analogue Life
愛知県名古屋市瑞穂区松月町4-9-2-2F
2F 4-9-2 Shogetsucho, Nagoya Mizuho-ku, Aichi
TEL090-9948-7163
http://www.analoguelife.com/

FRANK暮らしの道具 /
FRANK kurashi no dougu
岡山県岡山市中区平井1-1-13
1-1-13 Hirai, Okayama Naka-ku, Okayama
TEL086-238-8316
http://www.frank-dougu.com/

HANAわくすい / HANA-WAKUSUI
長崎県東彼杵郡波佐見町井石郷2187-4
2187-4 Isekigo, Higashisonogigun Hasamicho,
Nagasaki
TEL0956-85-8155
http://hanawakusui.jp/

照宝の中華蒸篭
Chinese Seiro (Chinese steamer) / Shouhou

照宝 / Shouhou
神奈川県横浜市中区山下町150
150 Yamashitacho, Yokohama Naka-ku,
Kanagawa
TEL045-681-0234
http://www.shouhou.jp/

ゆかい社中そらぐみの桶細工のおひつ
**Oke-Ohitsu (Wooden Container for Cooked Rice) /
Yukaishachu Soragumi**

jokogumo
東京都新宿区白銀町1-6
1-6 Shiroganecho, Shinjuku-ku, Tokyo
TEL03-5228-3997
http://jokogumo.jp/

OUTBOUND
東京都武蔵野市吉祥寺本町2-7-4-101
101 2-7-4 Kichijojihoncho, Musashino, Tokyo
TEL0422-27-7720
http://outbound.to/

まちのシューレ963 / Machino-schule 963
香川県高松市丸亀町13-3高松丸亀町参番街東館2F
Takamatsumarugamemachisanbangaihigashikan
2F 13-3 Marugamemachi,Takamatsu, Kagawa
TEL087-800-7888
http://www.schule.jp/

ゆかい社中そらぐみ / Yukaishachu Soragumi
徳島県徳島市新浜町4-1-39-2F
2F-4-1-39 Shinhamacho, Tokushima, Tokushima
TEL090-2895-3974
http://sora-dougu.jugem.jp

滴生舎の漆の器
Urushi Lacquerware / Tekiseisha

滴生舎 / Tekiseisha
岩手県二戸市浄法寺町御山中前田23-6
23-6 Jobojimachi Onyamanakamaeta, Ninohe,
Iwate
TEL0195-38-2511
http://www.tekiseisha.com/

**松屋銀座デザインコレクション /
Matsuya Ginza Design Collection**
東京都中央区銀座3-6-1
3-6-1 Ginza, Chuo-ku, Tokyo
TEL03-3567-1211(大代表)
http://www.matsuya.com/m_ginza/

d47 design travel store
東京都渋谷区渋谷2-21-1渋谷ヒカリエ8F
Shibuya Hikarie8F 2-21-1 Shibuya, Shibuya-ku,
Tokyo
TEL03-6427-2301
http://www.hikarie8.com/d47designtravelstore/

喜八工房の拭き漆の器
Fuki-urushi Lacquerware / Kihachi Kobo

喜八工房 / Kihachi Kobo
石川県加賀市山中温泉塚谷町イ323
i323 Yamanakaonsen, Tsukatanimachi, Kaga,
Ishikawa
TEL0761-78-0048
http://www.kihachi-web.com/

**金沢ひがし茶屋街漆器直売処
（喜八工房 金沢東山店）/
Kanazawa Higashichayagai Shikki Chokubaijo
(Kihachi Kobo Kanazawa Higashiyama Store)**
石川県金沢市東山1-26-7
1-26-7 Higashiyama, Kanazawa, Ishikawa
TEL076-251-1151

J-PERIOD
全国に店舗があるため、情報はホームページで
確認を。
Stores are located throughout Japan. Please visit
the website for more information.
http://www.j-period.com/jp/

BALS TOKYO
全国に店舗があるため、情報はホームページで
確認を。
Stores are located throughout Japan. Please visit
the website for more information.
http://www.balstokyo.com/jp/

久保一幸の竹の籠
Bamboo Basket / Kazuyuki Kubo

LIVINGMOTIF
東京都港区六本木5-17-1AXISビルB1F、1F、2F
AXIS Building B1F,1F,2F 5-17-1 Roppongi,
Minato-ku, Tokyo
TEL03-3587-2784
http://www.livingmotif.com/

秋篠の森 月草 / Akishino no Mori Tsukikusa
奈良県奈良市中山町1534
1534 Nakayamacho, Nara, Nara
TEL0742-47-4460
http://www.kuruminoki.co.jp/akishinonomori/

井山三希子の粉引・白マットの器
Kohiki and Matte White Ware / Mikiko Iyama

KOHORO
東京都世田谷区玉川3-12-11-1F
1F 3-12-11 Tamagawa, Setagaya-ku, Tokyo
TEL03-5717-9401
http://www.kohoro.jp/

Zakka
東京都渋谷区神宮前5-42-9グリーンリーブス
#102
Greenleaves102 5-42-9 Jingumae, Shibuya-ku,
Tokyo
FAX03-3407-7003
http://www2.ttcn.ne.jp/zakka-tky.com/

木と根 / Kitone
京都府京都市下京区燈籠町589-1-1F
1F 589-1 Torocho, Kyoto Shimogyo-ku, Kyoto
TEL075-352-2428
http://kitone.jp/

くるみの木cage / Kuruminoki cage
奈良県奈良市法蓮町567-1
567-1 Horencho, Nara, Nara
TEL0742-20-1480
http://www.kuruminoki.co.jp/

安藤雅信の銀彩の器
Silver Overglaze Ware / Masanobu Ando

ギャルリももぐさ / Galerie Momogusa
岐阜県多治見市東栄町2-8-16
2-8-16 Toeicho, Tajimi, Gifu
TEL0572-21-3368
http://www.momogusa.jp/

山本忠正の土鍋
Donabe Clay Pot / Tadamasa Yamamoto

ギャラリーやまほん / Gallery Yamahon
三重県伊賀市丸柱1650
1650 Marubashira, Iga, Mie
TEL0595-44-1911
http://www.gallery-yamahon.com/

**ギャラリーうつわノート /
Gallery Utsuwa-note**
埼玉県川越市小仙波町1-7-6
1-7-6 Kosenbamachi, Kawagoe, Saitama
TEL049-298-8715
http://utsuwa-note.com/

Analogue Life
愛知県名古屋市瑞穂区松月町4-9-2-2F
2F 4-9-2 Shogetsucho, Nagoya Mizuho-ku, Aichi
TEL090-9948-7163
http://www.analoguelife.com/

一陽窯の備前焼の器
Bizen Ware / Ichiyougama

一陽窯 / Ichiyougama
岡山県備前市伊部670
670 Inbe, Bizen, Okayama
TEL0869-64-3655
https://www.facebook.com/ichiyougama

ギャラリー栂 / Gallery Toga
岡山県和気郡和気町清水288-1
288-1 Shimizu, Wakegun Wakecho, Okayama
TEL0869-92-9817
http://gallerytoga.web.fc2.com/

成田理俊の鍛鉄のフライパン
Wrought Iron Frying Pan / Takayoshi Narita

夏椿 / Natsutsubaki
東京都世田谷区桜3-6-20
3-6-20 Sakura, Setaga-ku, Tokyo
TEL03-5799-4696

in-kyo
東京都台東区駒形2-5-1柳田ビル1F
Yanagida Building1F 2-5-1 Komagata, Taito-ku,
Tokyo
TEL03-3842-3577
http://in-kyo.net/

くるみの木cage / Kuruminoki cage
奈良県奈良市法蓮町567-1
567-1 Horencho, Nara, Nara
TEL0742-20-1480
http://www.kuruminoki.co.jp/

及源鋳造の南部鉄器
Nambu Ironware / Oigen Foundry

日本橋 木屋本店 / Kiya Nihonbashi Main Store
東京都中央区日本橋室町2-2-1コレド室町1F
COREDO Muromachi 1F 2-2-1
Nihonbashimuromachi, Chuo-ku, Tokyo
TEL03-3241-0110
http://www.kiya-hamono.co.jp/

私の部屋 / Watashi no Heya
全国に店舗があるため、情報はホームページで
確認を。
Stores are located throughout Japan. Please visit
the website for more information.
http://www.watashinoheya.co.jp/

山田工業所の中華鍋
Wok / Yamada Kogyosho

ナカタ / Nakata
北海道札幌市東区北14条東1
1 Kita14johigashi, Sapporo Higashi-ku, Hokkaido
TEL011-721-1331
http://www.sapporo-nakata.co.jp/

和田食器 / Wada Shokki
東京都渋谷区渋谷3-3-1
3-3-1 Shibuya, Shibuya-ku, Tokyo
TEL03-3400-2886
http://www.rakuten.co.jp/shokki

青木商事 / Aoki Shoji
神奈川県横浜市中区山下町133
133 Yamashitacho, Yokohama Naka-ku, Kanagawa
TEL045-681-5176

千田 / Senda
大阪府大阪市中央区難波千日前8-16
8-16 Nanbasennichimae, Osaka Chuo-ku, Osaka
TEL06-6632-5851
http://www.senda.co.jp/

生活春秋の無水鍋®
Aluminum Pot (Musuinabe) / Seikatsu Shunju

D&DEPARTMENT
店舗数が多いため、情報はホームページで確認を。
Stores are located throughout Japan. Please visit the website for more information.
http://www.d-department.com

212KITCHEN STORE
全国に店舗があるため、情報はホームページで確認を。
Stores are located throughout Japan. Please visit the website for more information.
http://www.212kitchenstore.com/site/

クロワッサンの店 / Kurowassan no Mise
全国に店舗があるため、情報はホームページで確認を。
Stores are located throughout Japan. Please visit the website for more information.
http://magazineworld.jp/special/croissant/shop/

東急ハンズ / Tokyu Hands
全国に店舗があるため、情報はホームページで確認を。
Stores are located throughout Japan. Please visit the website for more information.
http://www.tokyu-hands.co.jp/

松屋銀座デザインコレクション / Matsuya Ginza Design Collection
東京都中央区銀座3-6-1
3-6-1 Ginza, Chuo-ku, Tokyo
TEL03-3567-1211（大代表）
http://www.matsuya.com/m_ginza/

和田助製作所のステンレスの鍋
Stainless Steel Saucepan / Wadasuke Seisakusho

和田助製作所オンラインショップ / Wadasuke Seisakusho Online Shop
http://www.wadasuke.co.jp/

ニイミ洋食器店 / Niimi Yoshokkiten
東京都台東区松が谷1-1-14
1-1-14 Matsugaya, Taito-ku, Tokyo
TEL03-3842-0213

水野正美の銅の鍋
Copper Saucepan / Masami Mizuno

Farmer's Table
東京都渋谷区恵比寿南2-8-13共立電機ビル4F
Kyoritsudenki Building4F 2-8-13 Ebisuminami, Shibuya-ku, Tokyo
TEL03-6452-2330
http://www.farmerstable.com/

夏至 / Geshi
長野県長野市大門町54-2F
2F 54 Daimoncho, Nagano, Nagano
TEL026-237-2367
http://www.janis.or.jp/users/geshi/

THE SHOP十二ヵ月 / THE SHOP Jyunikagetsu
愛知県名古屋市中区上前津1-3-2村上ビル1F
Murakami Building1F 1-3-2 Kamimaezu, Nagoya Naka-ku, Aichi
TEL052-321-1717
http://jyunikagetsu.blog58.fc2.com/

くるみの木cage / Kuruminoki cage
奈良県奈良市法蓮町567-1
567-1 Horencho, Nara, Nara
TEL0742-20-1480
http://www.kuruminoki.co.jp/

野田琺瑯の琺瑯の鍋
Enamel Pot / Noda Horo

取扱い店は野田琺瑯へ問い合わせを。
Please contact Noda Horo.
http://www.nodahoro.com/

omoto 鈴木康人の鋼の包丁
**Hagane Hocho Knife (carbon steel knife) /
omoto Yasuto Suzuki**

かぐれ表参道店 / Kagure Omotesando
東京都渋谷区神宮前4-25-12 MICO神宮前
MICO Jingumae 4-25-12 Jingumae, Shibuya-
ku, Tokyo
TEL03-5414-5737
http://www.kagure.jp/

jokogumo
東京都新宿区白銀町1-6
1-6 Shiroganecho, Sinjuku-ku, Tokyo
TEL03-5228-3997
http://jokogumo.jp/

TAjiKAのステンレスのキッチンばさみ
Stainless Steel Kitchen Shears / TAjiKA

松屋銀座デザインコレクション /
Matsuya Ginza Design Collection
東京都中央区銀座3-6-1
3-6-1 Ginza, Chuo-ku, Tokyo
TEL03-3567-1211（大代表）
http://www.matsuya.com/m_ginza/

くらすこと / kurasukoto
東京都杉並区久我山2-23-29ハイネス富士見ヶ丘1F
Hainesufujimigaoka1F 2-23-29 Kugayama,
Suginami-ku, Tokyo
TEL03-5344-9715
http://www.kurasukoto.com/store/

Gloini
石川県金沢市長町1-6-16
1-6-16 Nagamachi, Kanazawa, Ishikawa
TEL076-255-0121
http://gloini.net/

Analogue Life
愛知県名古屋市瑞穂区松月町4-9-2-2F
2F 4-9-2 Shogetsucho, Nagoya Mizuho-ku, Aichi
TEL090-9948-7163
http://www.analoguelife.com/

まちのシューレ963 / Machino-schule 963
香川県高松市丸亀町13-3高松丸亀町参番街東館2F
Takamatsumarugamemachisanbangaihigashikan
2F 13-3 Marugamemachi, Takamatsu, Kagawa
TEL087-800-7888
http://www.schule.jp/

ラッキーウッドのシルバーのカトラリー
Silver Cutlery / LUCKYWOOD

ニイミ洋食器店 / Niimi Yoshokkiten
東京都台東区松が谷1-1-14
1-1-14 Matsugaya, Taito-ku, Tokyo
TEL03-3842-0213

ほか、取扱い店はラッキーウッドに問い合わせを。
Please contact LUCKYWOOD.
http://www.luckywood.jp

日野明子 (ひのあきこ)

ひとり問屋、スタジオ木瓜代表として、百貨店やショップと、作り手をつなぐ問屋業を中心に、生活に関わる日本の手仕事関連の展示や企画協力に携わる。松屋商事を経て1999年に独立し、ひとりで問屋業を開始。著書に『うつわの手帖1 (お茶)』『うつわの手帖2 (ごはん)』(共にラトルズ)、『台所道具を一生ものにする手入れ術』(小社)ほか、雑誌や新聞への寄稿も多数。

AKIKO HINO

As a director of one-person wholesaler Studio Boke, AKIKO HINO connects artisans with buyers from department stores and retailers. Akiko has been involved in various exhibitions and events promoting Japanese hand-made crafts and utensils for daily use. After working for Matsuya Shoji, she began her own wholesale business in 1999. Akiko has published "Utsuwa Techo 1 (Ocha)" and "Utsuwa Techo 2 (Gohan)" by Rutles, and "Daidokoro Dougu wo Isshoumononi Suru Teirejutsu" by Seibundo-shinkosha. Akiko also contributes articles to magazines and newspapers.

撮影/photographs 　有賀傑　金子睦
デザイン/design 　高橋克治 (eats & crafts)
編集/editing 　土田由佳
翻訳/translation 　鎌田裕子
英文校正/English editing 　江原健

撮影協力/Photo shoot locations
ヒトト (東京都武蔵野市吉祥寺南町1-6-7 3F
0422-46-0337　http://www.organic-base.com/cafe)
carta (岩手県盛岡市内丸16-16　019-651-5375　http://carta.blog.shinobi.jp/)

Japanese-English Bilingual Books

英語訳付き
ニッポンの台所道具と手入れ術
How to Care for Japanese Kitchen Utensils
受け継がれる職人・作家の手仕事

NDC597

2015年3月26日　発　行

著　者　日野明子
発行者　小川雄一
発行所　株式会社誠文堂新光社
　　　　〒113-0033　東京都文京区本郷3-3-11
　　　　(編集) 電話03-5800-3614
　　　　(販売) 電話03-5800-5780
　　　　http://www.seibundo-shinkosha.net/
印刷・製本　図書印刷 株式会社

ISBN978-4-416-71516-1

本書は、2014年6月に小社より刊行された『台所道具を一生ものにする手入れ術』の記事を一部抜粋し、英語訳を付けて再編集したものです。